DESIGN
THE LEADING HOTELS OF THE WORLD

DESIGN

THE LEADING HOTELS OF THE WORLD

Editorial Direction by The Slowdown

Spencer Bailey

Editor-in-Chief

Cynthia Rosenfeld

Executive Editor

Contents

Foreword

By Paul Goldberger

THE PARADOX OF HOTELS is that they need to feel like home and like the opposite of home at the same time. We want them to give us the comforts of home, to make us feel nurtured and cared for. And yet, that is never, of course, enough, since, unless your home happens to be a palace, you also expect a great hotel to transcend the associations you have with home and take you into another world, a world of elegance and sophistication, a world that shows you a whole other way to live. When a hotel is doing what it should, it can make you feel that it was designed for you and you alone, even as it is filled with the activity and energy of dozens, maybe hundreds, of other people, each of whom is also feeling that this place was made just for them. That is another part of the paradox: A great hotel is at once a celebration of private life and public life. It is where the intimate joys of privacy and the exhilarating pleasures of community come together.

It takes a lot of different factors to make this work, but it starts, most often, with architecture and design. We know what a hotel looks like before we have met anyone at the reception desk, or tasted the food, or swum in the pool. The design of a hotel carries much of this contradictory burden of making us feel at home while also putting home out of mind entirely. If the look of a hotel is too strange, it can be stressful and off-putting. But if it is too familiar, it will not transport us anywhere worth going at all.

The greatest hotels, many of which appear in this book, manage the difficult trick of caring for us and inspiring us, of making us simultaneously feel the calm of contentment and the thrill of the exotic. There is no single way that architects and designers achieve this, and they have been doing it both successfully and unsuccessfully for a long time. There are those great hotels like the Ritz Paris, where the genius of the architect Thierry Despont's 2018 renovation made it look as if nothing, or almost nothing, had been done, other than to make you think that the Ritz Paris was better than you had remembered it. Design, here, was in a million subtle details that gently reinterpreted the Ritz, which has always been an extraordinary combination of the intimate and the grand, at once a cloister and a palace. Despont understood this perfectly and knew that the secret of good design is in making the private parts of the Ritz feel grand, and the grand parts feel private, so that there is always an element of surprise.

Not everything that surprises you in a hotel is necessarily good, but everything good is almost always just a bit surprising, whether it's the rhythm of the curving shapes in the Foster + Partners–designed Capella Singapore, where an undulating modern form exists in counterpoint to a traditional colonnade, or the lightness of the modernism of Snøhetta's design for the Falkensteiner Hotel Montafon in Austria, where a (primarily) dark exterior belies the notion that transparency is the quickest way to connect architecture to nature. There is surprise, too, in the rich colors of the interiors of the Helvetia & Bristol, in Florence, reconceived by Anouska Hempel, whose rooms make you feel almost as if you were inside a painting, with precision and richness in perfect equilibrium. Precision also invokes surprise at The Okura Tokyo, where Yoshio Taniguchi has evoked the spirit of the original Okura—a midcentury masterpiece by his father, Yoshiro—the hotel that showed the world that the restraint of traditional Japanese architecture could be brilliantly expressed in modern form, and that minimalism could create a luxurious hotel. It was distressing, at first, to hear that the old (1964) Okura was to be replaced, but in the new version, completed in 2019, Yoshio seems mainly to bring it forward, honoring the past while subtly reinventing it, as Despont did at the Ritz Paris.

Many of the hotels in this book are restorations and reinterpretations of older places: The Newbury Boston by Jeffrey Beers, Alexandra Champalimaud, and Ken Fulk, which brings a soft, domestic luxury to the premises of its 1927 building; the classic Bairro Alto Hotel in Lisbon that was renovated by Eduardo Souto de Moura; The Dylan Amsterdam, a spare Dutch building elegantly reconceived by Studio Linse, with many of the rooms done in black and white; or L'oscar London, once a Baptist church and now

a hotel that pays flamboyant homage to Oscar Wilde with a design by Jacques Garcia that manages to feel slightly decadent and still more than a little bit dignified.

Every one of these places is different, a thing unto itself. That, of course, is what really marks a great hotel: that it is like no place else. Never mind that it is not like being at home—being in any one of these hotels is not like being in any other hotel either, because each place in the pages that follow has its own mark, its own character, its own way of making you feel content in its space. When a hotel is a great piece of design, it can make you feel textures and colors and light and space, perhaps with more intensity than you are accustomed to, and it brings these things together in a way that both energizes and relaxes you. It has a buzz, and yet it feels serene. It exudes a glow, a warmth, and while it is grand, it never overpowers you. Awe is not the goal of hotel design. Joy, and the gift of feeling welcome, is what hotels are made for.

Introduction

By Spencer Bailey

IN 1928, WHEN THE Leading Hotels of the World was founded by a group of 38 forward-looking hoteliers—all but one based in Europe—travel was dominated by trains and ocean liners. Fast-forward to the 1960s and '70s, though, and airlines had radically transformed the industry. LHW's founders foresaw this global shift and were ready for it: By the end of the 1970s, a decade in which The Leading Hotels of Europe (as LHW was originally called) became The Leading Hotels of *the World*, the collection had grown to 150 hotels in 32 countries, and by the turn of the 21st century, it was the largest group of independent hotels in the world. In our current era, with around 100,000 commercial airline flights traversing the sky each day, totaling more than 30 million per year—many to far-flung destinations that one could only have dreamed of visiting a century ago (Easter Island! The Seychelles!)—LHW encompasses more than 400 hotels across 80 countries, a collection of impeccably run properties, most of them multigenerational and family-owned and -operated, ranging from the Britannia Hotel in Trondheim, Norway (LHW's northernmost hotel), to the Arakur Ushuaia Resort & Spa in Argentina (its southernmost); from the Baglioni Resort Maldives on Maagau Island to the Halekulani on the Hawaiian island of O'ahu; from the Imperial Hotel, Tokyo, to The Ritz London.

This book—the first in a series of themed LHW titles edited, curated, and produced by The Slowdown; written by today's top travel, design, and culture journalists; designed by the award-winning firm Pentagram; and exquisitely published by Phaidon's Monacelli imprint—presents a selection of 74 LHW hotels that place a strong emphasis on design and illustrate how extraordinary aesthetics serve exceptional luxury hospitality. (Future titles will explore culture, wellness, gastronomy, and beyond.) Our goal for this book, and for the entire series, is to create a tactile, thoughtfully crafted experience that embodies the elegant essence of LHW and manifests, in printed form, the absolute magic of staying at any one of its hotels.

To achieve this, we dispatched writers and photographers around the globe. The book's executive editor, the Los Angeles–based journalist and travel-trade veteran Cynthia Rosenfeld, took off for Europe, where she stayed at both the serene, aptly named Botanic Sanctuary Antwerp (page 141) and the lavishly appointed La Réserve Paris Hotel and Spa (page 197). Another L.A.-based journalist, Janelle Zara, hopped in her car and drove to Sedona, Arizona, where she reveled in Ambiente, A Landscape Hotel (page 25). In Milan, the local design curator and author Maria Cristina Didero immersed herself in the neighborhood- and city-defining Portrait Milano (page 231). And I flew over to Japan, where I found myself utterly enraptured by The Okura Tokyo (page 103).

Elsewhere in the book, we meet up with two pairs of cultural mover-shakers for conversations at two LHW properties: the fashion designer Carla Fernández and the architect Michel Rojkind at Casa Polanco in Mexico City (page 35), and the fashion designer Gabriela Hearst and the chef Daniel Humm at The Greenwich Hotel in New York City (page 45). At once heady and handy, these enlivening dialogues explore their shrewd perspectives on their respective home cities and also include a few favorite "insider" addresses to visit.

The book's Index (pages 261–283), which is organized alphabetically by country, presents the entire LHW collection in all its glory, with more handpicked tastemaker advice—all of it with a particular bent on design. Among the recommendations are the sculptor and ceramicist Simone Bodmer-Turner's preferred Paris haunts, the architect Stephanie Goto's Kyoto and Tokyo tips, the hotelier Marguita Kracht's number one architectural destination in Zurich, and the Milan-based architect and designer Paola Navone's agenda for Athens.

What surprised me most in putting this book together was the incredible breadth and depth of LHW's collection when examined through a design lens. Featured within are three hotels with designs by the Pritzker Prize–winning architect Norman Foster—Capella Singapore (page 91), The Dolder Grand in Zurich (page 158), and the Kulm Hotel St. Moritz (page 191); three more by the highly sought-after Belgian-born, Malaysia-based designer Jean-Michel Gathy—The Chedi Muscat in Oman (page 14), The Setai, Miami Beach (page 78), and The Chedi Andermatt in Switzerland (page 157); as well as one—the Bairro Alto Hotel in Lisbon (page 129)—designed by yet another Pritzker winner, Eduardo Souto de Moura. Viewed as a whole, the entire LHW portfolio could be considered a veritable A to Z of many of today's, well, leading architects and designers, from Jonathan Adler to Mario Botta, from Jacques Garcia to Jacques Grange, from Snøhetta to Philippe Starck, from Yoshio Taniguchi to Patricia Urquiola, from Isay Weinfeld to Yabu Pushelberg.

In the case of the majestically minimalist Soori Bali (page 119), its architect, Soo K. Chan, is also the owner; the same goes for the Vinha Boutique Hotel in Vila Nova de Gaia, Portugal (page 255), co-owned by architect Joana Poças, who overhauled a 16th-century manor house into a fetching, fashion-forward property. Behind two perfectly outfitted penthouse suites in the book—one in The Greenwich Hotel, the other atop the Bayerischer Hof in Munich (page 132)—is the legendary Belgian interiors maestro and antiques dealer Axel Vervoordt. And at The Newbury Boston (page 69), one of the book's most star-studded affairs, three interior-design giants—Jeffrey Beers, Alexandra Champalimaud, and Ken Fulk—gracefully reimagined a stately landmark property built in 1927.

Although LHW, to some, may be synonymous with Old World European élan—and there are indeed dozens of hotels in the collection that exemplify such grandeur, including the Grand Hotel Principe di Piemonte in Viareggio, Italy (page 175) and L'oscar London (page 194)—this book lays out an expansive, otherworldly view of hospitality design, one full of sumptuous surprises and alluring details at each turn. It's my hope that it serves not only as a travel guide and a helpful reference, but also as an enlivening showcase of some of the most exceptionally designed hotels in the world, inside and out, near and far.

Africa
& the
Middle East

The Chedi El Gouna, Red Sea

Red Sea, Egypt

El Gouna, the city built by the Egyptian-born Montenegrin investor Samih Sawiris atop desert sand, spreads across 20 islands in lagoons along the Red Sea Riviera. A kitesurfer's paradise, the place takes its name from the Masri term for "the lagoon."

In 2022, at Sawiris's invitation, the Singapore-based GHM Hotels opened The Chedi El Gouna, Red Sea along a private cove in this flourishing oasis. For this Chedi outpost, the brand's Asian, meditative identity is immediately conveyed through the double-height, linear teak arrival pergola. Inside, a sense of place manifests in the desert foliage bas-reliefs, colossal Egyptian marble discs, and mother-of-pearl inlaid furniture in the low-lit lobby. Beyond, blush and burnt-orange buildings linked by curved archways take architectural cues from the region's Nubian and rural heritage, sharing the manicured grounds with clusters of desert palms. Elongated jade fronds flap in the warm, oud-scented sea breeze.

Rome-based interior designer Elisabetta Freda transposed the desert's serene palette into the 82 guest-room interiors, adding black-and-white photographs of old Cairo, chess sets carved with pieces depicting King Tutankhamen and the cat goddess Bastet, and the crisp cotton bed linens for which Egypt is renowned. Garden suites open onto wide terraces while beachfront accommodations practically touch the sand. This intimate connection to its surroundings extends to the hotel's refined dining options: Around half of the three restaurants' ingredients come from local farmers, including succulent fruits from the Nile Valley.
—**Cynthia Rosenfeld**

The Chedi Muscat

Muscat, Sultanate of Oman

Where the Hajar Mountains meet the Gulf of Oman on this country's northern coast, the Belgian architect Jean-Michel Gathy took inspiration from Bedouin tents for The Chedi Muscat, which sits along a 1,257-foot (383-meter)-long private beachfront just four miles from Sultan Qaboos Grand Mosque. Doormen in traditional Omani dress, down to the khanjar daggers at their waists, greet guests in the heavily draped lobby hung with Asian-inspired lanterns. Outside, the landscape architect Karl Princic encircled the exceptionally appointed Moorish water garden with lush date palms and endemic Emirati flower beds.

Following months spent studying the area's traditional architecture, Gathy designed the 21-acre (8.5-hectare) property around a series of fountains, courtyards, and waterways inspired by the Omani *falaj* system that for centuries carried fresh water from underground wells. One hundred sixty-two high-ceilinged rooms and suites inhabit one-, two-, and three-story buildings embellished with Islamic arches, domes, and *mashrabiya* screens. In these restrained retreats, illuminated by pendulous lanterns, polished mahogany wood dramatically juxtaposes the stark white walls. Each features a low-slung Omani divan and windows overlooking gardens, mountains, or the Gulf. Suites incorporate sunken black terrazzo bathtubs and sea-facing terraces. The property also includes six restaurants designed by Yasuhiro Koichi of Design Studio Spin, among them the outdoor Shisha Courtyard, with its intimate nooks designed for passing around traditional water pipes; three swimming pools, including the lengthiest one in the Middle East, at 338 feet (103 meters); and a spa with Asian-leaning therapies such as Balinese massage and Ayurveda. —**C.R.**

The Chedi Muscat

La Mamounia

Marrakech, Morocco

First opened in 1923 and located within the ochre-hued clay walls of Marrakech's medina, the 209-room La Mamounia marked its 100th anniversary with renovations that balance tradition with modernity. Designed by the Parisian firm Jouin Manku, the hotel's refresh blends Moorish, Moroccan, and Art Deco styles.

Etched metal lanterns hang above the main entrance, with its Zellige-tiled columns and hand-carved, delicately painted mosaics. Passing through the stained-glass doors, visitors encounter an homage to contemporary Moroccan craftsmanship in the colossal "Centenary Chandelier" suspended across the Grand Hall, its crisscross of red strands affixed with 650 pure-silver Berber adornments and surrounded by ribbed glass thread from the Czech lighting manufacturer Lasvit. The adjacent alcoves evoke the intimacy of an oasis, with velvet Moroccan sectional *sedari* sofas, cultural ephemera, and backlit *mashrabiya* panels.

Named for the former British prime minister, who was a frequent guest, Le Churchill bar recalls a Pullman carriage in its narrow proportions and curved ceiling. In the colonnaded Pierre Hermé tea salon, a contemporary, conical glass chandelier overhangs Jouin Manku's minimalist take on the Moroccan courtyard fountain. Of the hotel's two Jean-Georges Vongerichten restaurants, the more informal L'Italien conjures a winter garden, with its walls of windows, olive-green textiles, and whimsical tropical frieze by the artist Cédric Peltier, while the noted French lighting designer Stéphane Carratero subtly illuminates each individually lacquered dining table at the romantic L'Asiatique. Next door, in the plum-carpeted Majorelle Lounge, cocoon-like chairs and banquettes orient visitors toward the hotel's legendary 20 acres (8.1 hectares) of palm-dappled gardens. —**C.R.**

Acqualina Resort & Residences on the Beach
Sunny Isles Beach, Florida

Americas & the Caribbean

Acqualina Resort & Residences on the Beach

Sunny Isles Beach, Florida

If one were to fly overhead along South Florida's Sunny Isles Beach, an impressive array of hibiscus-red umbrellas, loungers, and sunbeds splayed across the white sand would unabashedly announce the Acqualina Resort & Residences on the Beach. Set on nearly five acres (two hectares) between Miami and Fort Lauderdale, the sprawling property is completely open to the ocean, free of barriers between the 51-story tower and its 400 feet (122 meters) of pristine shoreline.

Decked out with five Baroque fountains, limestone balustrades, colonnade walkways, marble statues, a bell tower, a domed cupola, and stately iron gates that guard the piazza-esque porte-cochere, it's no secret that architect Robert M. Swedroe's palatial design was informed by larger-than-life European ideas of grandeur. Swathed in hues evoking the emerald green waters of the Atlantic, the contemporary gallery lobby, designed by STA Architectural Group, conveys a worldly glamour, with its eight arched windows, Fendi Casa furniture, bespoke hand-tufted Nepali rugs, white- and silver-leaf-accented chandeliers, and custom-pearlized Venetian stucco wall treatments.

After a dip in the ocean or in one of the hotel's three oceanfront swimming pools, guests can retire to a space outfitted by the celebrated Miami designer Isabel Tragash, who infused the 54 guest rooms and 44 suites with sun-bleached shades of gray, taupe, and sand. Channel-tufted walnut wraparound headboards, Italian-made sofa beds, wingback chairs, and silky satin fabrics imbue each room with an aristocratic flair. Once replenished, guests can step out to the bougainvillea-adorned and brass-accented Avra, the Miami outpost of the much-lauded Greek restaurant group, for Kaluga caviar or freshly flown-in filets of branzino and black sea bass. **—Emily Jiang**

Ambiente, A Landscape Hotel

Sedona, Arizona

Text by **Janelle Zara**
Photography by **Elizabeth Daniels**

At Ambiente, A Landscape Hotel, each room is referred to as an "Atrium," a standalone, cube-shaped villa that hovers on stilts above the rocky land. In the evenings, below the star-covered remote desert sky, these Atriums glow like enormous lanterns through walls of floor-to-ceiling glass. In the daylight, when the cloudless Sedona atmosphere turns crystal blue, these exquisite windows look out onto towering red-rock formations—with quirky names including Steamboat, Snoopy, and Coffee Pot—that line the horizon like rows of ancient towers.

Sedona is a small, central Arizona town located a two-hour drive north of Phoenix. Over the course of millions of years, the area's shifting tectonic plates slowly but diligently forced the land upward, each layer of sediment forming horizontal striations that mark the passage of time. Erosion caused by wind, rain, and

Previous spread
The "Atriums"
at Ambiente, A
Landscape Hotel,
with Brins Mesa
in the distance.

Opposite
Ambiente's heated
pool and spa, with
views of Mitten Ridge
beyond.

snowmelt carved these protrusions into canyons and buttes, and oxidized the iron-rich stone that turned the landscape its brilliant shade of rust.

Although Sedona's year-round population stands at only about 10,000 people, these rocks attract upwards of three million visitors annually, a mix of outdoorsy types drawn to the Coconino National Forest's 90-some hiking trails and New Age gurus seeking spiritual invigoration. In the late 1970s, local legends of mysterious fonts of supernatural energy, or vortexes, began to emerge, giving life to an economy of crystal shops, psychic readers, and other destinations for holistic wellness.

Whether or not you believe in vortexes, the magic of the land itself is the focal point of the Ambiente experience. The hotel's owners, sisters and Sedona natives Jennifer May and Colleen TeBrake, bought their three-acre (1.2-hectare) plot in 2015 with visions of foregrounding Sedona's natural beauty. They took inspiration from the landscape hotels that had emerged throughout Europe, a style that blends luxury hospitality with cozy, minimalist architecture built around existing topography to emphasize spectacular views of the natural surroundings. Looking to build the first such landscape hotel in North America, they commissioned two firms: the Sedona- and Del Mar, California–based Stephen Thompson Architect Studio, a specialist in environmentally harmonious desert-locale projects, and the Phoenix-based ASUL Architects, known for crafting modernist, steel-framed structures, and raising them above the ground on piers.

In 2021, Sedona became the second resort town in the United States to join the Global Sustainable Tourism Council, an international network committed to upholding standards of environmental protection. As such, May and TeBrake's proposal resonated particularly with Sedona's City Council for its sensitivity to the landscape. Rather than flattening the hilly site to make room for an enormous new building, they planned to construct individual accommodations poised just above the ground, lessening their impact on the environment. According to the architects, roughly 90 percent of the existing shrubbery and other vegetation remains untouched.

The resulting Atriums, 40 in total, mark a slick departure from the textures typical of the local architecture; in Sedona, buildings overwhelmingly embrace a Southwestern heritage, drawing references to adobe construction and Spanish missions, or the distressed wooden siding of an Old West saloon. But at Ambiente, each boxlike structure is clad in charcoal-colored, corrugated-metal walls, and appears to float just above the rocky terrain. As freestanding buildings, they dot the property like the homes of an environmentally sensitive residential neighborhood, connected by walkways that surround a central lagoon-like pool. Naturally, the owners rotated each room so as to catch the best views through bronze-tinted floor-to-ceiling windows. In the daytime, from the outside, the glass catches reflections of Sedona's immaculate blue sky and rust-colored landscape.

The adults-only property provides a sense of being both well cared for and surrounded by nature, with alternating experiences of adventure and relaxation. The hotel offers mountain biking, transportation, and private tours on which guests can explore Sedona's 400 miles

Americas & the Caribbean

Opposite, top to bottom
Each Atrium features floor-to-ceiling wrap-around windows for unobstructed Sedona or resort views.

Ambiente's indoor-outdoor restaurant, Forty1, features leather banquette seating and mirrored views of the surrounding landscape.

(644 kilometers) of pristine hiking trails. Just alongside the hotel's entrance is the mouth of the moderate Adobe Jack Trails. Spending the day indoors, however, is also an enticing prospect. May and TeBrake designed each 576-square-foot (54-square-meter) room with an array of plush textiles in a neutral palette; their idea was to create a clean-lined interior that emphasizes the expansive views, like the screen of an IMAX theater. Live-edge wood furniture warms the space, alongside generous touches: an ample sofa in the living area, an oversize black bathtub, and a frequently replenished, complimentary minibar that functions more like a small kitchen.

Within each Atrium, a plush king bed faces motorized blackout curtains that open to reveal those 180-degree views that originally compelled the owners to create this property. The walkways connecting each Atrium are scored by birdsong, as well as the gentle babbling of rushing water. The landscape architects at Krizan Associates, along with the team at Green Magic Landscaping, activated Ambiente's wash, a normally dry creek bed that fills with water during seasonal rains, by irrigating the property's own well. The recirculating stream runs clear without the use of chemicals, just the natural filtration of aquatic plants and continuous movement.

At Forty1, the on-site restaurant and the 41st building on the property, the charcoal-gray interiors are lined with a lush leather banquette and the golden glow of a full, warmly lit bar. It's also possible to take breakfast outdoors, sitting poolside, where the kitchen operates inside a converted Airstream trailer. The servers generously offer suggestions for exploring Sedona. There's Tlaquepaque, a small village of artisanal shops and art galleries styled like an old Spanish hacienda, or hiking to the Boynton Canyon Vortex, where the tree trunks mysteriously grow in a spiral. Throughout your hikes, you're bound to encounter a few group meditations along the trails.

For me, the highlight of Ambiente was my Atrium's spacious private sky terrace, designed to capture the surrounding mood and atmosphere, which evolved by the hour. During the day, I soaked in the blazing desert sun, and at night, after enjoying a roaring fire and the thick extra blanket provided in the room, I retreated to the roof to look up at the vast constellations of stars. Basking in the owners' vision of creating a scenic escape within one of only 44 certified International Dark Sky Communities in the world, my favorite time was late in the afternoon, as the sun sank below the rusty spires and the sky faded momentarily to the same golden color as the rocks, before cooling to a dusky purple, and finally, to black.

This page
Ambiente sits on three acres (1.2 hectares) along the Coconino National Forest.

Opposite
A fountain and spiral staircase featuring large chimes greet guests at the entrances to the Velvet Spa.

Opposite
A network of streams
flow around the resort,
finding their way
to the main lagoon
before the water is
recirculated back
to the top of the
property.

This page
An Atrium, as seen
from outside at night.

Ambiente, A Landscape Hotel

Casa Polanco

Mexico City, Mexico

In Conversation **Michel Rojkind & Carla Fernández**
Photography by **Ogata**

REFLECTIVE OF MEXICO CITY'S VIBRANT, cosmopolitan culture, Casa Polanco is located in the city's upscale Polanco neighborhood, across the street from Parque Lincoln—a lush green space featuring an aviary, a pond, and an open-air theater—and a short stroll from many of the city's best restaurants, bars, and fashion boutiques. A sanctuary of a hotel within an oasis of a neighborhood, it was originally built as a private residence in the 1940s and underwent a four-year restoration and expansion before opening in 2022. Inside, there's a reading room bedecked with custom wood furniture by Héctor Esrawe, a carefully curated book selection, and a complimentary bar cart that welcomes guests upon entering; beyond it is the hotel's check-in desk and La Veranda restaurant and "social space." The 19 generously proportioned rooms and suites, lined with walnut floors and filled with bespoke furniture, feature tailor-made textiles, paintings by the artist Jordi Boldó, and various artworks by the Huichol people. On the roof is a private gym and spa.

The hotel is a fitting place for the fashion designer Carla Fernández and the architect Michel Rojkind to connect. When the two greet each other inside the Neoclassical manor, it's with a casualness so striking that it seems as if they're meeting up at a friend's house or somewhere they've been countless times before. Which isn't entirely far off: While this is their first time stepping through the hotel's front gate, both Fernández and Rojkind know Casa Polanco's owner, Octavio Aguilar, and went to university with the hotel's architects, Claudio and Christian Gantous. (Mónica Romo and Monica Novelo, the mother-daughter team behind the firm Casa M+M, oversaw the hotel's interiors.)

Among the biggest names and most important voices in Mexico City's thriving design scene, Fernández and Rojkind are longtime friends who have known each other since they were students together at the Universidad Iberoamericana in the early '90s, and have seen each other's creative practices evolve significantly over the decades. Fernández, whose upbringing was steeped in Mexican culture (her father was the director of the museums within Mexico's National Institute of Anthropology and History), became an expert in Mexican textiles and went on to launch her cult-favorite namesake fashion label in 2000. During his architecture studies, Rojkind was the drummer in one of Latin America's most popular rock bands at the time, Aleks Syntek y La Gente Normal. In 1997, after an eight-year run in the band, he left to pursue an architecture career full time. Both Fernández and Rojkind bring an open-armed and -minded, collectivist, and decidedly Mexican approach to their respective creative practices: Her brand is dedicated to preserving and revitalizing the textile legacy of Indigenous and *mestizo* communities of Mexico; he designs bold, inventive, neighborhood-defining buildings, including Mexico City's Cineteca Nacional (2014) and Veracruz's Foro Boca concert hall (2017), that invite in the communities they serve.

Meeting up in the hotel's Lincoln Suite, Fernández and Rojkind discuss Mexico City's richly layered cultural scene; the vast, transformational changes they've witnessed across the city over the past three decades; and why the city serves as an ideal hub for creativity and design.

Michel Rojkind It's an honor to have known you for so long, Carla, and to have seen your career flourish. I'm a huge fan of you and Pedro [Reyes, Fernández's artist husband] as creatives, but also as human beings. I love the family that you have, and your kids. But back in the day, did you ever imagine where you would be today?

Carla Fernández Well, I think you and I have something in common: Work and passion are what drive us, and we don't think about being "successful" or not. We think of doing the things that we *want* to and that we love. The paths we take are like a river. The water flows and you just have to let go. But I imagined I was going to be a creator, not only creating things, but also

making statements about what I thought was needed in the world. For me, in those days—and still now—we needed to have a Mexican fashion industry that was not necessarily happening.

Tell me, in Mexican architecture in those days, what was happening? How do you see it today?

MR In Mexico, at least in our generation, we were taught to be like [the Mexican architect Ricardo] Legorreta. We had been through the times of Mario Pani and Luis Barragán and all these other architects who did all these impressive modernist projects. Legorreta was the next influence. So, in schools, we were taught to be like Legorreta: pink, bright colors. It was awful,

"In Mexico, we're incredibly creative and ingenious by necessity. It's so incredible when you think about it, all the creative spectacles happening here." **Michel Rojkind**

Previous spread
Michel Rojkind, left, with Carla Fernández in the library room at Casa Polanco in Mexico City.

This page
The hotel's front gate and signage.

because we wanted to express ourselves very differently from him. I've always been grateful to the generation of Enrique Norten and [Alberto] Kalach—these architects who really fought to reintroduce modernism to Mexico, in order for our generation to be able to express ourselves in the ways we would go on to.

CF Your generation of architects is very strong. I think you are *the* generation, or one of a couple of generations, that have changed the landscape of Mexico City and other places.

It was much more difficult for fashion. We had amazing fashion designers, but not that many, and none as recognized outside Mexico as our architects.

MR There was no industry for fashion, first of all. You were solving the idea of manufacturing, but also understanding what fashion is. I've always loved the way you've had a statement— you've always been very political. I always say that, whether you like it or not, *everything* is political. You can design something and say you're not political, but you're saying something anyway, so you might as well make it something that you're fighting for.

In Mexico, we're incredibly creative and ingenious by necessity. Mexicans are ingenious because they need to figure out how to survive and how to strive. They're finding creative ways to make a living in the street. It's so incredible when you think about it, all the creative spectacles happening here in the city from sunrise to sunset. We're not expecting a system to solve things, as in many other countries. Here, there is no system, so you have to go out and make things happen.

CF Well, Mexico is one of the most diverse countries in the world in terms of cultural differences. We have sixty-eight different languages. It's almost as linguistically rich as China and India. Compared with the size of those two countries, our country is much smaller. Also in terms of biodiversity, Mexico is very complex. This is the richness of our country.

Mexico was the center of the world when the Spanish came. The *galeóns* would come from Asia, stop in Manila, and from there go to Acapulco, and then through Puebla, Oaxaca, et cetera, and go and cross Veracruz to go to Spain and to Europe—and the other way around. So you have all these items coming from Europe, crossing to Mexico. That's why you can find *mole*—it's the thing we have that most resembles curry. Or you have flowers from China and the laces of Belgium. This complexity gave us that richness.

MR I find it incredibly chaotic here. In a way, you *have to* be creative around the chaos. Because we're not expecting a system to solve things in a certain order, we improvise. I remember when Nina, my daughter, was growing up, and I had to show her how to walk. We were walking, and when she went from the sidewalk to the street, I would tell her, "Look, Nina, in other countries, when the green light is green, you only look on one side, because you know that the cars are coming from left to right. Here in Mexico, if you put your foot on the street, you look to your left, you look to your right, you look up and you look down, because anything can come from anywhere." It's a certain awareness. To me, at least in my upbringing as a designer and creative person, this was beautiful.

CF I've always lived in Downtown Mexico City, and earlier in my life, my parents were living in Condesa, so that's where I grew up. The city has changed quite a bit. There were two restaurants in my neighborhood and no schools, so I had to travel far away to get to school. In 1985, Roma had an earthquake, so a lot of people moved out from that neighborhood and Condesa. Nowadays, it's like being in—

MR Williamsburg [in Brooklyn].

CF Yes. Downtown was not as vibrant when I was young as it is now. Its current rise started in the late nineties. The nineties were a very strange time here. Mexico was always looking to the north, and we wanted to be part of that development. We wanted to be part of the "American dream." Today, we thank the universe that that didn't happen.

MR What's interesting to me—and I always try to explain this to my friends who live elsewhere—is that I've always seen a creative community trying to show a Mexico that's not the Mexico people hear about in the news. There's you doing fashion, Héctor [Esrawe] doing industrial design, Alejandro González Iñárritu doing films, Enrique Olvera doing food.

Yes, we have insecurity. Yes, we have inequalities. It's very hard here in many ways, but there are also all these beautiful creative voices that I think have made Mexico what it is today. We were talking about Roma and Condesa, and how they now look like Williamsburg, because when people who came here as digital nomads during the pandemic realized the richness of our country, they stayed. That, to me, has been the most interesting recent change.

But that's been the history of how many artists have been living here in Mexico for years, because they came for a couple of weeks and then they decided to stay forever. Or some were immigrants that were invited by architects. I remember Mario Pani inviting the architect Vladimir Kaspé here. Kaspé was a Jewish immigrant. Pani was like, "Come to Mexico, you'll be fine here!" Mexico has always been a place that receives foreigners, and when they come here, they stay. This has made Mexico much better.

CF That's true. We are a superpower in terms of cultural identity.

MR Let's talk about Polanco. I lived here for ten years when I was with [my ex-wife]. Living here was really interesting at that moment because it felt like a small neighborhood, even though Polanco has always been a little bit disconnected from everything else happening in Mexico City, because you have the embassies and Chapultepec Park here. It's kind of a little bubble in itself. It's not like Condesa or Roma,

where you have the metro system. Polanco is a little bit isolated. There are always the same people in the restaurants here. Everybody knows each other because they all go to the same park. It was a great place to live at the moment my daughter was born, because I could walk to the park and do all these things outside with her. I think Polanco is a beautiful neighborhood because it's very walkable. For running, I would just walk to Chapultepec Park and run from there.

It was also incredible to see these old houses around here that were refurbished. Casa Polanco is a great recent example of this: a hotel preserved inside an existing house with this beautiful addition by Claudio and Christian Gantous. They're great designers.

CF What have you designed in this neighborhood?

MR The Japanese restaurant Tori Tori (Temístocles 61).

CF I had my first store here in Polanco, on Avenida Moliere. The design of the store was by Pedro Reyes, my husband, and Jorge Rubia, this friend of ours. I remember Pedro made a beautiful mural for it out of staples. Everything was so carefully done. I think it lasted for four or five years. But for me, I was more used to a neighborhood with the openness of Condesa or Roma. I felt a bit like an outsider in Polanco.

But that's what's nice about Mexico City: You have not only the different architecture, and the different options for eating, but each neighborhood has a different vibe. In this neighborhood, you have the most beautiful museum in the world, the Museo Nacional de Antropología (Av. P.º de la Reforma s/n).

MR You also have the Auditorio Nacional (Av. P.º de la Reforma 50). You have all of the museums in Chapultepec—the Museo Tamayo (Av. P.º de la Reforma 51), the Museo de Arte Moderno (Av. P.º de la Reforma s/n). In terms of the richness of culture, Polanco is amazing. And Polanco keeps

**This page,
left to right**
Fernández in
conversation, with
an artwork by Jordi
Boldó behind her.

The front door of
Casa Polanco, with
artworks by the
Mexican photographer
Graciela Iturbide on
either side.

"For me, one of the biggest gifts is when someone asks me, 'What do you think is the greatest asset of Mexico?' I think it's that we're very friendly and curious." **Carla Fernández**

This page, clockwise from top left
A table setting inside La Veranda restaurant and "social space."

A staircase inside the hotel.

The second-floor landing, above the lobby and check-in desk.

PARK VIEW

Americas & the Caribbean

on growing. There's this new high-density zone that they kind of invented out of nowhere that's called the "New Polanco."

This area is definitely a beautiful place to live. It's like living around Central Park in New York, with the park right in front. And as with Central Park, which has the Guggenheim and the Metropolitan Museum of Art, here you have Antropología, Tamayo, and all these other beautiful museums in the park.

CF For restaurants in Polanco, I recommend Masala y Maíz (Calle Marsella 72) and Ticuchi (Petrarca 254). I have a very good relationship with the chefs at Masala y Maíz, Norma Listman and Saqib Keval, who I think are amazing, mixing Asia with San Francisco with Mexico. I love the food there.

MR Pujol (Tennyson 133), as well.

CF Yes, but for me, Ticuchi is better—it's vegan. And Contramar (Calle de Durango 200) in Roma Norte. It's very much like being at home.

MR I always describe Contramar as the "contemporary cantina." It's like the typical cantina that we used to have here. There are still a couple of old ones that survive, but I think of Contramar as the contemporary version, where politicians are there on a Thursday and then everybody's flirting on a Friday.

I've always called Mexico City the "eight-headed monster," because it has all these different neighborhoods. Somehow, if you're here, it's great, and there, it's great. Connecting from this neighborhood to that neighborhood, just be careful. But once you're in a neighborhood, you have this incredible vibe that's palpable and human-scale. In the south of the city, there's San Ángel, which has a nice scale, but if you leave San Ángel—again, a little bit of chaos. Each area has its beauty.

The first thing I ask people coming to Mexico City is, "How many days do you have?" At least one place that I always send people to is the National Autonomous University of Mexico (Av. Universidad 3004, Copilco Universidad, Coyoacán), in the south of the city. That campus!

CF Yeah, it's beautiful. As you were saying, you have to plan your visit to Mexico City by region.

For me, one of the biggest gifts is when someone asks me, "What do you think is the greatest asset of Mexico?" I think it's that we're very friendly and curious. We like to ask questions, and we like to learn. We also like to share, like, "Oh yeah, *this* is how we do it." It's very welcoming here.

MR I always joke that we open up our houses to anybody who comes from outside Mexico. We're like, "Come on in!"

Here in Mexico, the waiters are nice—you can tip them or not tip them, they don't care—and if you don't want something in a restaurant, you can actually ask if they can change it or mix it, or take these ingredients out. In other parts of the world, the restaurant would typically say, "No, there's no way we can do that." Here, they go for it. Going back to Contramar, this restaurant by Gabriela Cámara that we love, it's the most extreme example of this high level of service. I think there are more waiters than diners in that restaurant. You feel super taken care of there.

CF *Cherished.*

MR Really, you can go to any part of Mexico—not only Mexico City, any part of Mexico—and always feel welcome.

The Greenwich Hotel

New York, New York

In Conversation **Gabriela Hearst & Daniel Humm**
Photography by **Ogata**

LOCATED IN NEW YORK CITY'S Tribeca neighborhood, The Greenwich Hotel—an 87-room property conceived by Ira Drukier and Robert De Niro, along with their partners Richard Born and Raphael De Niro—has a subtle, elevated, and highly refined approach to design and service. The building's bespoke furniture, rich material palette (handmade bricks from Pennsylvania, custom cast bronze medallions, reclaimed wood, salvaged door pulls, antique glass, Turkish travertine, Moroccan tiles), and other expertly crafted touches together make for one of Manhattan's coziest hotels. Staying here is truly a home-away-from-home experience. (Pro tip: Order a cocktail at the ground-floor Drawing Room—which features a library and exquisitely designed bookshelves—and sink into one of its velvet or leather couches.)

Imagined as an artist's atelier, one of the property's two duplex suites, the homey Greenwich Duplex Suite, features a 30-foot (9.1-meter)-high skylight, a full kitchen, two primary bedrooms, two bathrooms, a stone fireplace, and an office with a separate entrance. Just above it, on the top floor, is the crown jewel of the hotel: the impeccably appointed, 6,800-square-foot (630-square-meter) Tribeca Penthouse, designed by Axel Vervoordt and the architect Tatsuro Miki, who applied the ancient Japanese aesthetic philosophy of *wabi* to form this meditative lair. Combining antique and custom-made fixtures and furnishings, the space features a living room, a drawing room, a kitchen, three bedrooms, two and a half bathrooms, three fireplaces, and a 4,000-square-foot (372-square-meter) terrace with wisteria-wrapped pergolas and a spa pool.

For the Uruguayan-born fashion designer Gabriela Hearst and the Swiss-born chef Daniel Humm, The Greenwich Hotel is a natural meet-up spot. Humm, it turns out, has previously had an extended stay in the Greenwich Duplex Suite, and Hearst eats at the Locanda Verde restaurant downstairs with some regularity. When the two Manhattanites walk into the Greenwich suite, there's a palpable warmth between them. Ever since meeting, in 2018, they've been incredibly close, and both are at the peaks of their professional fields: Humm is the chef-owner of the three-Michelin-starred restaurant Eleven Madison Park (EMP) in Manhattan, and Hearst, the recipient of many awards (including a C.F.D.A. Womenswear Designer of the Year honor), runs her own namesake fashion label, one of the top independent luxury brands in the world.

Their worldviews and bold leadership perspectives are highly complementary, too. Humm co-founded the nonprofit Rethink Food, whose mission is to reduce food insecurity, provide meals for local communities, and rescue excess food, and he made headlines when he switched EMP, long known for its meat and fish staples, to a vegan, plant-based menu in 2021, citing the climate crisis as a key reason. Hearst's brand is widely respected for its unusually high level of quality, sustainability practices (she presented the industry's first carbon-neutral runway show), and philanthropic giving (for multiple years in a row, she has donated weeks of sales proceeds to the humanitarian organization Save the Children). Through their approaches to their respective crafts, both have risen to become prominent and vital voices in what could be called "climate-forward luxury."

Sitting down for a literal fireside chat, Hearst and Humm discuss their deep friendship, their personal views on creativity and leadership, and why New York City is their "favorite place in the world."

Gabriela Hearst I absolutely love this hotel, and I especially love the sheep's-milk ricotta and truffle honey they serve at Locanda Verde.

Daniel Humm I love being here, too. This place feels like it's been here forever. Maybe not quite, but it's definitely been here as long as I've been living here. This hotel has a great energy. I like sitting downstairs. Once, when I was renovating an apartment, I stayed in this very suite for a while.

GH This place has *character*. It feels like being at home.

DH For me, that's what great hospitality is about: how you feel. You might not remember what you ate or what you drank, but you will always remember how someplace or someone made you feel. The Greenwich Hotel has that.

GH Yeah. To me, hospitality is making people feel welcome, comfortable, and themselves—

"To me, hospitality is making people feel welcome, comfortable, and themselves— and giving them something nice to drink and to eat." **Gabriela Hearst**

This page, from top
Hearst in conversation in the Greenwich Duplex Suite.

One of the two bedrooms inside the Greenwich Duplex Suite.

and giving them something nice to drink and to eat.

Speaking of hospitality, do you remember when we met, judging that travel award competition? I was so busy, and was like, "What is this thing I have to do? I'm not sure I want to do this...."

DH It was the same for me. I didn't want to go.

GH I had no idea who you were, but when we were judging together, I realized I loved your taste, your vision, your humor.

DH We even left together that day. The whole thing felt—

GH Like a dream. We laughed a lot. We met just as you had closed Eleven Madison Park, right after you got to number one in The World's 50 Best Restaurants list.

DH I think what we do is very similar: the work intensity, the managing of teams, having to be creative, working on a seasonal calendar. I've never met anyone who works harder than you.

GH I feel the same way about you. This friendship, the intensity—it's *family*. It's deep respect and admiration for you as a human, for what you achieve, your vision, your execution. Against the advice of anyone, when you see something you want, you go for it. I've seen you in your ups, downs, ups, downs. And it's just remarkable, because that's when you really *see* someone. Life is not this constant success story, going up, up, up.

DH We've seen each other through the—

GH Pandemic. Your restaurant was closing. I could ship things online. But for you the music stopped from one moment to another, without you knowing if you were ever going to open again. Decades of work, of building a team.

DH Sometimes, the top is a very lonely place to be. As good as a team you have, there are certain things that are hard to share—you can't really expect your team to be in it as much as you are.

GH There's that great Kendrick Lamar song, "Crown," that references the line "heavy is the head that wears the crown." So, it's great to have those people around who will challenge you, who will tell you the truth, who will be like, "Snap out of it!" Nobody does anything alone.

DH To me, it's always about the artist's experience to read the world at a particular time, and then create something as a response to it. I'm no climate expert, but my decision [to turn EMP] into an entirely vegan, plant-based restaurant comes from my response to where we are as a world and to what I've seen with my eyes. Certain ingredients are no longer available.

GH The scarcity of quality.

DH This situation has made us both react. I see that in you, too.

GH The way business is currently being done, it's a no-go. We're both trying to prove a new model of how this can be done today. For Gabriela Hearst the company, this has been done with a long-term view and sustainability. I truly believe we're one of the few true luxury companies in the world because we use top, prime materials.

As long as we're moving this world eighty percent on fossil fuels, we don't have a chance. Fusion energy is where my mission has taken me. Your journey as a chef is the same as mine in fashion, to show that it's common sense. You know your materials the same way a designer does. You saw the decrease in quality of the ingredients, so you asked, "What am I going to do?" The answer was plants.

DH Yeah. When Eleven Madison Park became the number one restaurant in the world, the view wasn't that great, to be honest. These awards motivate you and your team, and they're very powerful because they're measurable. But the energy to reach these awards fades and becomes less meaningful. Even how you communicate to your team where you're going next, it's not easy.

When the pandemic hit, all of a sudden we had no business. We were facing bankruptcy; we couldn't pay our rent or our employees. At times, I didn't even know if I wanted to reopen the restaurant again. Now there's a new chapter, which I started with Rethink Food, and feeding people in need. I felt like, Wow, this work really matters. I'm making a difference. I felt more connected with the language of food. I also felt much more connected with New York City. I went to neighborhoods I'd never been to before. I wasn't sure where to take Eleven Madison Park next, but being the number one restaurant in the world had given me a voice, and it became clear that I wanted to use that for the betterment of people and the planet.

GH Let's talk about our favorite place in the world: New York. We're the biggest lovers of New York. How many times have you told me that New York is the greatest city? I mean, I'll go to Madrid and eat all the *jamón*—without you, Daniel, obviously. [*Laughs*] But New York vibrates differently. I can be exhausted traveling for work, but when I put a foot in New York and sleep, I'm fine.

DH You're switched on immediately here. When I first moved here, there was a time when I thought, Wow, this city is going to exhaust and overwhelm me. I'm going to age so quickly because the pace is so fast and intense. But actually, I think the speed and intensity of New York keeps you young.

GH What are some of your favorite places in the city? Mine's Kinokuniya (1073 6th Avenue), the Japanese bookstore near Bryant Park. I go there for pens, pencils, books, everything. I've been taking my kids there for years.

And pizza—Daniel, you and I have different views on pizza places. Tell me your favorite.

DH Have we had it together?

GH Yeah, L'Industrie (254 South 2nd Street, Brooklyn).

DH And what happened? It didn't change your life?

GH I like it, but I don't know if I want to do that extra distance from Scarr's (35 Orchard Street). I love L'Industrie, but I don't know if it's worth the trip to Brooklyn. [*Laughs*] Scarr's is pretty good, but for you, it's a bit too greasy. I get it. I also love JG Melon (1291 3rd Avenue) and, of course, Eleven Madison Park (11 Madison Avenue).

DH There's also Hangawi (12 East 32nd Street), a Korean plant-based restaurant in Koreatown. You sit in these little recessed chairs, low to the table. It's incredible.

GH Where else? I love the Museum of Natural History (200 Central Park West). A lot of New York has to do with food for me, but the planetarium at the Museum of Natural History, I love as an experience.

DH In terms of art, New York is just unbelievable. We've got the Metropolitan Museum of Art (1000 5th Avenue) and the ever-changing shows at MoMA (11 West 53rd Street) and the Guggenheim Museum (1071 5th Avenue), and then there are all the galleries.

The thing I love about New York, too, is that if you're doing something that is truly of worldwide importance, eventually you're going to pass through New York. Everyone we're inspired by or look up to eventually passes through our city. Being here, it's never-ending inspiration.

GH Yeah, it's really multicultural—a melting pot. I've noticed something happens to you on the street here. Immediately, New Yorkers are ready to help you. We have a reputation of being cold and toughies, but at the same time, we're there for each other. In every single crisis that New York faces, you can never bet against

"If you're doing something that is truly of worldwide importance, eventually you're going to pass through New York. Everyone we're inspired by or look up to eventually passes through our city. Being here, it's never-ending inspiration." **Daniel Humm**

This page, clockwise from top
The minimalist living room of the Tribeca Penthouse, designed by Axel Vervoordt and the architect Tatsuro Miki.

A fireplace in the Tribeca Penthouse.

A bedside table in the Tribeca Penthouse.

New York—it always comes back. It has an energy that's truly remarkable.

DH I actually think New Yorkers are very friendly. I know for some people there's this reputation that that's not the case. But I think it's one of the friendliest cities in the world.

GH We don't have a "This table's mine!" attitude here.

DH Yes, it's a positive place. Everyone's looking for solutions.

GH People come here to *work*. It's not a leisure city. This is not an easy place, exactly.

DH You move to New York because you want to accomplish something. It's the best place for that.

GH The beauty of New York, you only see it when you're outside, because from the inside, it's not actually that gorgeous. Let's be real. But then, when you return and see the skyline, you're like, "Oh man, I live there, this crazy place!"

When I get away, I have one place I love the most: an island in Greece. I'm so ecstatically happy there. You know how people always say that in a past life they were a king or an emperor or a queen, or a knight or a warrior? I know I was a Greek goat, because I'm so happy going up and down the hills where my house is. I do that twice a day, and it's bliss. I go down, I come up, say good day, say good night.

DH I've been traveling to Europe so much throughout my life, and I love it there. The south of France, Switzerland, those cultures really feel like home. But lately, since I started changing the restaurant to being plant-based, and researching all these ancient cuisines from all over the world that are, and have been, much more plant-based than European cuisine, I've loved traveling in India. Forty percent of India's population is vegetarian. I've also loved going to Japan and Korea, visiting the temples.

I've found this new interest in the world because of what we're doing in the restaurant. I think plant-based cooking is much more open to the world. To find inspiration, my travels are taking me to many different places than I was going before. I feel the shift in the restaurant because of this.

We recently celebrated twenty-five years of Eleven Madison Park, and I feel so blessed that I've been there for twenty of those years. But after all this time, I think my excitement has never been bigger for the work, and for the restaurant, and for the research, than right now. I feel so invigorated.

The Hazelton Hotel

Toronto, Canada

On a leafy corner in the heart of Yorkville, home to many of Toronto's best museums, including the Art Gallery of Ontario, the Royal Ontario Museum, and the Bata Shoe Museum, and just minutes on foot from the city's upscale "Mink Mile" shopping district, the 62-room, 15-suite Hazelton Hotel is outwardly unassuming, but inside, it's all opulence. In keeping with its cultured surroundings, the hotel's public areas feature a gallery of (mostly) Canadian art, with pieces by the likes of Hunt Solnen, Cynthia Chapman, and Paul Rousso.

Completed in 2008 as one of the earlier projects of the prolific Toronto- and New York-based firm Yabu Pushelberg, the hotel received a renovation and refresh by the studio in 2019. Its rich palette, plush velvet textures, brass accents, and custom furnishings, as well as new inviting nooks for moments of reflection, convey both the change in times and Yabu Pushelberg's evolution. Rooms, meanwhile, exude 1940s Hollywood grandeur, most notably in the generous green marble bathrooms and the balconies, which in warmer months are perfect for observing the street life below.

The global menu at One Restaurant, a seductive, low-lit space of slate grays, olive greens, and wood accents, complete with a wrap-around, candlelit patio, reflects the wanderings of executive chef Darby Piquette, who regularly changes the menu to reflect the seasons. Together with an inviting saltwater lap pool, a spa by the Swiss skin-care stalwart Valmont, and a state-of-the-art cinema named after the local movie mogul Norman Jewison, who also founded the Canadian Film Centre, the hotel gives guests persuasive reason to stay in and order room service.

—Warren Singh-Bartlett

The Hazelton Hotel

Hotel Las Majadas

Pirque, Chile

For those venturing out to Chile's Maipo Valley—a lush, expansive wine-growing region at the foot of the Andes—Hotel Las Majadas offers a rejuvenating stay that has long been enjoyed by presidents and princes alike. Along the edge of a private 20-acre (8.1-hectare) park designed in 1909 by Guillermo Renner runs the 656-foot (200-meter)-long linear structure of the hotel, which, with pauses and bends to accommodate the trees, positions all 50 rooms facing the park. The site's trifecta is completed by a centenary French-style palace by the architect Alberto Cruz Montt (1879–1955), an exponent of Neoclassical style known for designing many of Santiago's landmarks, including Palacio Eguiguren and Palacio Íñiguez.

Built by Lyon Bosch Arquitectos in 2015 according to strict design guidelines established to ensure that the project would enhance rather than interfere with the historic park, the hotel beautifully blends in with its surroundings. Elevated by a field of discreet concrete pillars and slabs, the building allows tree roots to thrive freely below and sits atop a ground level of open-air common spaces. Its cedar-colored, shutter-like façade, meanwhile, camouflages the structure with the surrounding trees. Woods from holm oaks and elms that fell naturally in the park are incorporated into exterior elements as well as interior furniture, giving the hotel an organic feel that helps dissolve the line between inside and outside. Each room, clothed in mid-toned paneled wood, translucent taupe curtains, and sage accents, features floor-to-ceiling, wall-spanning windows that open onto balconies overlooking a sea of green. **—E.J.**

Le Sereno Hotel, Villas & Spa

Saint Barthélemy

Tucked into a coveted Caribbean marine reserve known as Grand Cul de Sac—a crystal-clear lagoon teeming with swaying coral reefs, gliding sea turtles, and schooling fish—is Le Sereno Hotel, Villas & Spa, stretched across 600 feet (183 meters) of powder-white shoreline. Originally opened in 2005, the resort underwent a total rebuild in 2018 following Hurricane Irma. The restoration, inspired by the hotel's original design by master minimalist Christian Liaigre, saw the use of locally sourced materials such as coral stone and hardwood to create a piece of contemporary architecture that seamlessly blends with its surroundings. Beyond the breezy reception hut, for example, coconut palms encircle a heated freshwater pool that appears to become one with the sea, kept separate from it only by a thin wall lined with green stone tiles imported from Indonesia.

Inside the 39 suites and three villas—all situated at sea level—clean lines, simple forms, and a natural color palette of dark wood floors and bare white walls conjure an aura of utter tranquility. Dressed in D. Porthault linens, Kvadrat curtains, Kettal fabrics, Bonacina 1889 chairs, and both new and restored Liaigre furnishings, the suites feature floor-to-ceiling windows, private terraces, and verdant gardens by the Venezuelan landscape architect Enrique Blanco. After a day spent snorkeling, diving, or exploring the microregion's biodiversity, guests can dine on freshly caught fare at the open-air Le Sereno Al Mare Restaurant, designed by Liaigre and Patricia Urquiola and helmed by the chefs Raffaele Lenzi and Davide Mosca—the latter of whom comes from Le Sereno's Italian sister property, Il Sereno Lago di Como (page 184)—while still keeping their toes in the sand. **—E.J.**

Le Sereno Hotel, Villas & Spa

Nayara Bocas del Toro

Bocas Del Toro, Panama

Sixteen overwater villas feature at the lush Nayara Bocas del Toro on Frangipani Island in Panama's Bocas del Toro archipelago. Nesting along the shore, each one required more than 1,000 hours of work to finish, including the crafting of elaborate canopies, known as Balinese *tupong sari*, that hang over every bed.

The all-inclusive, adults-only property is also known for its unusual beach, a man-made, 90-foot (27-meter)-long area that sits on stilts over the water like a roofless bungalow, with steps down into the sea as if it were a swimming pool. Guests dipping in the water are likely to encounter remarkable marine life, as the crystal-clear sea teems with fish. And the land is not to be ignored, either: This resort is set in more than 80 acres (32 hectares) of mangrove forest along with nine acres (3.6 hectares) of dry land, and the paths that quilt the landscape lead to a delightful network of hidden gardens and ponds that appear, as if conjured from thin air, amid the dense thickets.

The water bungalows here were joined by four treehouses 50 feet (15 meters) up in the jungle canopy, the brainchild of the Bali-based designer Elora Hardy (daughter of the jeweler John Hardy), who tapped artisans from the Indonesian archipelago to work on the spaces. These three-story suites were built mostly from locally sourced and harvested materials, specifically wood dredged from the flooded forests that were submerged during the construction of the Panama Canal. There's more to that approach than sustainability: Wood hardens over time in those conditions, weathering and strengthening at the same time, making it a more durable choice for building in such tropical climes. A night can be spent here floating over the water or in mid-air.
—**Mark Ellwood**

Nayara Tented Camp

La Fortuna de San Carlos, Costa Rica

The 37-room Nayara Tented Camp nearby Costa Rica's Arenal Volcano reinvents the idea of glamping. Its air-conditioned, tented accommodations are artfully designed to combine the best of indoor and outdoor living. Note the steam trunk–like amenity stations, which open up like mirrored leather jewel boxes, complete with coffee maker and minibar; plus, the outdoor double-headed shower; and toiletries decanted into small ceramic jugs. On the private terrace of each room, alongside a snooze-ready hammock, there is an infinity-edge plunge pool—the best place to linger and contemplate the stark outline of the volcano on a clear sunny day.

The suspended bridge that connects many of the tents to the main building is a charming touch and the ideal spot for a souvenir snap or two. Guests shouldn't forget to take home one of the little stuffed animal sloths left as a turndown gift and in tribute to the resort's unofficial mascot, Tony, who's also depicted on the bas-relief carvings on each room's wooden door. There's even a sloth sanctuary on site, and a concierge on hand to help locate the real-life Tony on a walk through the jungle.

There's plenty more to this property than animal-friendly eco-mindedness: Owner Leo Ghitis is a prosocial entrepreneur who understands sustainability in the round rather than focusing solely on single-use plastic. To that end, he's building a staff village nearby, which he will sell to employees via subsidized mortgages. It's the ultimate attempt to combine minimal impact on the landscape from the resort, which is artfully jigsawed into the jungle, and maximum impact on locals' quality of life. —M.E.

Nayara Tented Camp

The Newbury Boston

Boston, Massachusetts

Set in Boston's historic Back Bay, just steps from the picturesque Public Garden and near the Boston Common, The Newbury Boston opened in 2021 inside a landmark property built in 1927. A trio of design partners—Champalimaud Design, Jeffrey Beers International, and Ken Fulk—creatively reimagined these 286 rooms and shared spaces as a stylishly contemporary sanctuary in one of the city's most established neighborhoods.

From the ground-floor lobby, with its Nero Dorato marble floors and rosewood reception desk, to the Art Deco rooftop restaurant, Contessa (a sister to New York's Carbone), this reinvented Neoclassical structure remains a vibrant hub for Bostonians and tourists alike. Lounge areas feature sumptuous seating in jewel-toned velvet and buttery leather, while The Street Bar, a clubby space with dark-wood panels, green leather banquettes, and leather armchairs, invites guests to sip classic cocktails fireside. Ken Fulk infused the 4,000-square-foot (372-square-meter) glass rooftop restaurant and Riva yacht–inspired bar with his characteristic theatrical flair, from the dusty rose banquettes and teal upholstered chairs to retro fringed chandeliers.

The tranquil guest rooms are the work of Champalimaud Design, which applied a soothing palette of grays, creams, and blues, as well as subtle textures, plus limestone and wood finishes. Forty-two of the 90 spacious suites are endowed with wood-burning fireplaces, serviced by fireplace butlers who deliver the guest's choice of four fragrant wood varietals (regular guests know to ask for the Newbury blend). Original artwork by illustrator Veronica Lawlor and herringbone wood floors are just a few more of the elegant touches that give this hotel its Old World European elegance and modern New England charm. —**Christina Ohly Evans**

Nine Orchard

New York, New York

Manhattan's Lower East Side has long been synonymous with experimental subcultures and unequivocal coolness while simultaneously preserving much of its historical flavor. Set near Dimes Square, the über-fashionable micro-neighborhood, and housed in a 1912 Beaux-Arts building originally erected by the architects Rouse & Goldstone as the Jarmulowsky Bank, Nine Orchard serves as a high-level paradigm of this confluence of the new and old, of the trendy and timeless. Unoccupied since 2006, the 14-story property's overhaul in 2022 preserved many of its essential neo-Renaissance characteristics, from its pearly limestone façade and vaulted ceilings to its original 60-foot (18-meter) rooftop *tempietto*—a delicate spired cupola—and inlaid, backlit clock that beams down on passersby.

Inside, the 113 guest rooms, designed by Reza Nouranian and owner Andrew Rifkin in collaboration with the Los Angeles–based gallerist Ray Azoulay, delight with details including antique French desks, vintage 1970s chrome chairs, original moldings, and weighty olive-green curtains that frame oversize windows. Bespoke floral-headboard beds by BDDW's Tyler Hays look onto lively artworks by the likes of Louise Bourgeois, Julie Mehretu, Raymond Pettibon, and Robert Rauschenberg, while custom speakers by Ojas transmit playlists curated by Devon Turnbull and D.J. Stretch Armstrong. Downstairs, the former bank teller's hall was transformed into the swank Swan Room cocktail bar, which is warmly lit by giant chandeliers and features mirrored geometric tables and powder-pink and vermilion booths. After a drink, guests can scooch over to the Corner Bar restaurant, and enjoy upscale New York favorites such as oysters and steak tartare. **—E.J.**

Parker Palm Springs

Palm Springs, California

A 23-foot (seven-meter)-high brise-soleil wall greets Parker Palm Springs's guests upon arrival, sheltering the 144-room hotel's entrance from the city's radiant sunshine and discreetly signaling the privacy that is a hallmark of this secluded desert oasis. Burnt-orange doors open to reveal a wonderland of old Hollywood opulence and eccentric glamour. In advance of its 2004 opening (the building dates to 1959), the renowned American designer Jonathan Adler—best known for his maximalist eponymous home décor line—furbished the hotel from head to toe in his signature color-bursting, over-the-top style. Adler's inspiration for the Parker's interiors, where vintage treasures mix with contemporary *objets*, furnishings, and textiles of his own design, was the home of an imaginary great aunt "who traveled the world and had great panache."

The hotel is housed on a 13-acre (5.3-hectare) estate that features lush tropical gardens designed by Judy Kameon of the Los Angeles-based firm Elysian Landscapes. Native plantings and heritage rose gardens encircle a croquet lawn that doubles as a romantic wedding locale. The property also includes 12 private villas and the two-bedroom Gene Autry Residence (once home to the actor, singer, and composer, who was also known as the "Singing Cowboy"), as well as a pétanque court, saltwater pools, a giant chessboard, and red-clay tennis courts. Also nestled within the Parker's grounds is the nautical-themed Palm Springs Yacht Club spa, which features an indoor saline pool.

Adler, whose trademark touches span two decades on the property, again gave the Parker a refresh in 2017, and in 2023 he transformed the guest baths into sumptuous sanctuaries that round out the hotel's alluring aesthetic.
—**Brooke Hodge**

Rock House

Providenciales, Turks and Caicos Islands

Ask Mark Durliat, the principal and CEO of Grace Bay Resorts, what he hoped to achieve when he opened this hotel on the north shore of Providenciales, and he'll answer, simply: to bring the Mediterranean to the Caribbean. Durliat and his television-producer wife, Melissa, lived and worked in the south of France for several years, and felt a kinship with the rocky cliffside here. They resolved to replicate that vibe—albeit with a spritz of year-round Caribbean warmth—back in Turks and Caicos Islands.

Rock House sits in an impressive spot, the highest on the island, and far quieter, too, than the necklace of resorts strung together along Grace Bay. The name of the 14-acre (5.7-hectare), 51-key property is an explicit nod to its painstakingly crafted architecture, for which slabs of limestone were excavated and carefully hand-carved before being assembled by local artisans into the low-slung block buildings, walkways, and walls that sit amid the surrounding greenery. There's an emphasis on natural materials throughout, particularly heavy on macramé and Eucalyptus bamboo. The long wooden jetty, jutting out 130 feet (40 meters) into the water, is a prime daytime perch, ideal for lazing on one of the loungers arranged along it.

The menu at the on-site Vita Restaurant remixes Italian dishes with a Caribbean twist, such as locally caught snapper *acqua pazza* and a lemon spaghetti upgraded with local lobster. The real draws, though, are Cave Bar and Sunset Bar. As their names suggest, one features a backdrop assembled with cavelike rocks and sits on the oceanfront, practically perfect for late-night D.J. dance parties, while the other overlooks the water in a sundowner-ready spot. —M.E.

The Setai, Miami Beach

Miami Beach, Florida

First opened in 1936 as the Dempsey-Vanderbilt Hotel, then reimagined in 2005 as The Setai, Miami Beach, this hotel revives one of the city's oldest Art Deco buildings with a minimalist, Asia-influenced touch. Dreamed up by the Malaysia-based Belgian architect Jean-Michel Gathy and the Indonesian interior designer Jaya Ibrahim, the design preserves the original rectilinear façade along Collins Avenue, with its distinctive floral bas-reliefs, zigzags, and chevrons, while introducing interiors that reference the flourishing 1930s Art Deco era in Shanghai. Imported antique gray bricks salvaged from Shanghainese lane houses comprise the ground-level flooring, walls, and area around the central fireplace. Outside, Jaya restaurant's dining nooks encircle the vast open-air courtyard's palm-fringed reflecting pool.

Along with three pool villas, the hotel features 91 rooms in the original building, plus 62 in the 40-story tower addition. In the former, a pared-back aesthetic incorporates sandstone-colored walls; black stone–edged teak floors; dark, earth-hued furniture; and original Asian antiques. In the latter, Ocean Suites feature Thai silks, contemporary art from Asia, and floor-to-ceiling windows that soak up the South Beach sunlight.

The Bar, with its handmade Burmese teak lattice cabinetry and mother-of-pearl mosaics, is where those in the know order the Indian *thali* plate. Inside the sensuous space are paintings by the Shanghai-based French artist Christian de Laubadère and the Korean artist Lee Jung Woong, and a serene, Sukhothai-style Thai Buddha carved in stone. A sculpture depicting Khmer ruler Jayavarman VII, the great Angkorian temple builder, watches over the Ocean Grill, created with Design Studio Spin. —**C.R.**

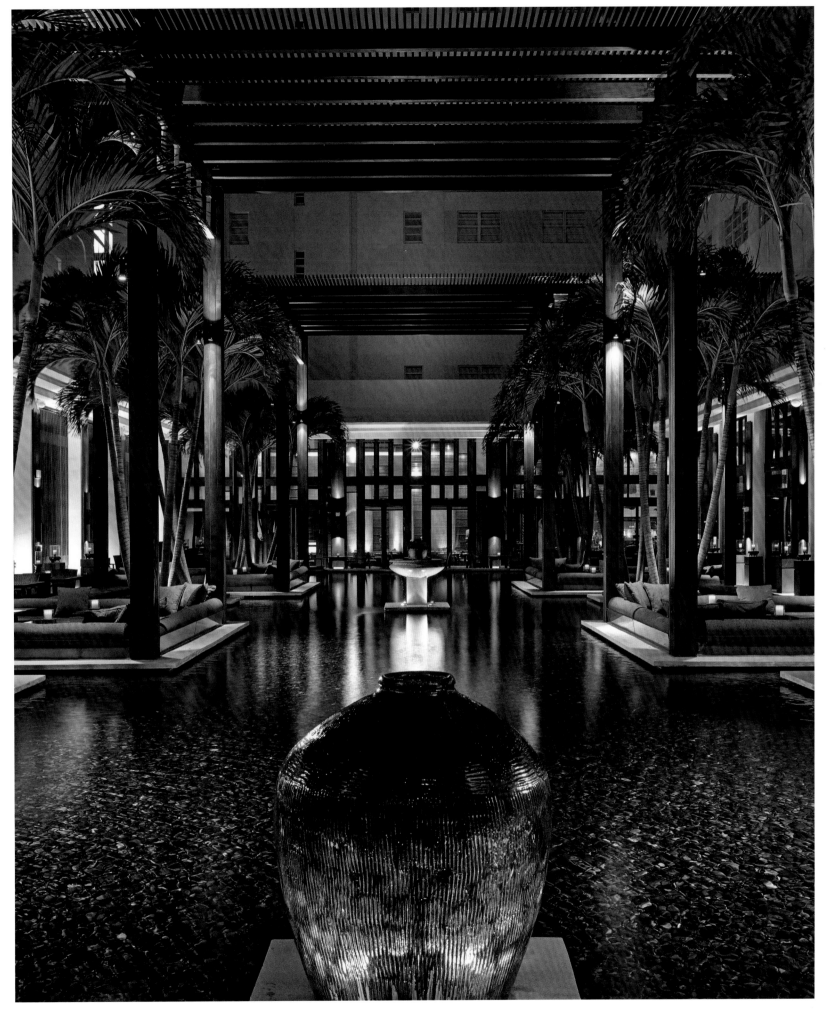

The Setai, Miami Beach

Silversands Grand Anse

St. George's, Grenada

The anchor of Silversands Grand Anse is its infinity pool—at 330 feet (100 meters), it's the longest in the Caribbean, and runs through the heart of the property like a catwalk, the ideal perch on which to idle away a day or two on the island. Indeed, when the hotel opened here, in 2018, it was the first high-design property in the country, commandeering a prime spot at the northern end of the best spit of sand, Grand Anse Beach. The infinity pool leads right out to the ocean there, presenting swimmers with a difficult choice.

Owner Naguib Sawiris, an Egyptian telecom titan, tasked Parisian design duo AW² with imagining the sleek, Saint-Tropez-meets-Spice-Island décor here (the jazzy, laid-back soundtrack playing throughout the space is also clearly intended to draw comparisons to the Côte d'Azur). Wandering around the villas or by the pool, it's plain to see that the French designers have emphasized a muted subtlety, all limestone terraces and pebbly black paths, a refreshing rebuttal to the clichés so commonplace in tropical design. Note, too, the artwork throughout, which Sawiris personally curated from his collection.

There are 51 rooms, including eight standalone villas that look out to the sea, as well as a pair of restaurants, one focused on local fare—the fresh-squeezed juices at breakfast are must-tries—and the other on Asian fusion. A snifter at the Puro lounge is the perfect way to round out the day. Guests can pair a cigar from one menu with rum from another—perhaps a Cohiba Siglo III with a shot of aged Black Tot Demerara from Guyana. **—M.E.**

The Singular Patagonia, Puerto Bories Hotel

Puerto Natales, Chile

On the remote outskirts of Puerto Natales in southern Chile, along the shores of the Señoret Channel and near Torres del Paine National Park, architect Pedro Kovacic and interior designer Enrique Concha radically transformed a former cold-storage house—a vestige of the British Empire that operated between 1915 and 1971—into The Singular Patagonia, Puerto Bories Hotel. This museum-like hotel, which opened in 2011, is drenched in history.

Guests descend from a promontory via a vintage funicular, then step onto a glass platform that reveals the triple-height, exposed-brick walls and steel beams of the main restaurant below, where wooden tables and pedestal lamps complement the original space's pipes and pulleys. Fittingly, the menu honors the area's history with dishes such as lamb sweetbread with sliced apple in thyme sauce. A former blacksmith's forge serves as the site of the second restaurant, called El Asador, which specializes in fire-grilled meats. More of the past is on display off the lobby, in the cavernous, Victorian-era engine room with its two enormous wood- and coal-fired boilers; the tannery; and the blacksmith shop, each filled with original tools and machinery.

For the accommodations, Kovacic affixed a three-story annex to the redbrick heritage structure (it was declared a national monument in 1996), blending the two with a pared-down design ethos that leans on exposed concrete and local woods. This setup—as well as the 19.7-foot (six-meter)-wide, floor-to-ceiling windows in each of the 54 guest rooms and three expansive suites—keeps the focus on the nearby Última Esperanza, or "Last Hope" Sound, and beyond, the Andes Mountains. **—C.R.**

The Singular Patagonia, Puerto Bories Hotel

Tivoli Mofarrej São Paulo

São Paulo, Brazil

Fortress-like at street level, the Brutalist concrete façade of the 218-room Tivoli Mofarrej São Paulo, pierced by rows of narrow, double-height oval portals, gracefully cantilevers out over the pool terrace above. Built by the Lebanese-Brazilian real estate titan Nabil Mofarrej (1917–1988), the 23-floor tower is a landmark in "S.P."—as the city is known by native Paulistas—and for good reason. From its magnificent spaceport-meets-greenhouse lobby, featuring a stunning chandelier by local sculptor Yutaka Toyota, to Estúdio Penha's revamped Presidential Suite—the largest in Latin America, with lamps by Jader Almeida, stools by Sergio Rodrigues, and armchairs by Percival Lafer, creating an alchemy of antique and midcentury Brazilian design—to the guest rooms, where the original interiors by Patricia Anastassiadis, the architect responsible for this harmonious ode to aggregates, remain intact, it impresses at every turn.

The hotel's exceptionalism extends to the food. Guests can enjoy cocktails by the celebrated mixologist Adriana Pino at the poolside Must Restaurant, then, at sunset, linger over the views from the 23rd floor at Seen Restaurant & Bar while exploring Franco-Portuguese chef Olivier da Costa's menu. In the heart of the city, close to the financial district and the boutiques on Rua Oscar Freire, as well as Lina Bo Bardi's landmark Museum of Art of São Paulo and Kengo Kuma's Japan House, the Mofarrej not only captures São Paulo's dizzying evolution, it's also a microcosm of the spirit of Brazil itself. —**W.S.B.**

UNICO 20°87° Hotel Riviera Maya

Riviera Maya, Mexico

The coordinates don't give much away, but the UNICO 20°87° Hotel Riviera Maya, a serene, adults-only Mexican seaside resort, lies somewhere north of tranquility and west of relaxation, its 448 expansive rooms housed in a horseshoe of beachfront buildings. The work of New York–based firm AvroKo, the pared-down rooms, with their contemporary four-poster beds, are dressed in cooling shades of gray and white and maximize views of the grounds, the pools, the Caribbean Sea, and the swaying palms—for some, courtesy of standalone tubs on the balconies; for others, from swim-up-pool level. The public areas, designed by Mexico City design firm Artigas, feature vaulting roofs, wood shutters, water fountains, potted palms, and wrought-iron pendant lamps, and elaborate on the modern hacienda style of rooms, localized by the inclusion of spectacular Mayan art pieces.

UNICO 20°87° is all-inclusive, and offers a wide variety of culturally minded experiences, including chocolate-making under the guidance of in-house chocolatier Sóol; tours of Chichen Itza; and trips to nearby cenotes, ethereal cave pools where the Mayans were said to commune with the underworld. These activities can be arranged by an army of *anfitriones*, local hosts who ensure that stays go smoothly. They do everything from arranging treatments at the Esencia Spa to booking tables at the five in-house restaurants—the modern Mexican at Cueva Siete, where staples such as the humble bean, corn, and chili are taken to sophisticated heights, and Mura House, where the hibachi offerings are of particular note—and will happily arrange entrance to the most in-demand spots elsewhere on the Riviera Maya. **—W.S.B.**

UNICO 20°87° Hotel Riviera Maya

Asia,
Australia
& the
Indian Ocean

Capella Singapore

Sentosa Island, Singapore

Norman Foster retrofitted two *Tanah Merah*–style 1880s buildings, originally constructed for British military officers on Singapore's Sentosa Island, creating this city-in-name-only hotel—his first in East Asia—in 2009. The island, mostly covered by a rainforest and home to monitor lizards, long-tailed macaques, parrots, and peacocks, inspired the architect to extend the colonial vernacular with deep, sheltered walkways that resemble existing 19th-century colonnades, terra-cotta-tiled roof canopies, and horizontal brise soleils. Foster's modern additions extend unbroken from each side of the existing structures, curving around a leafy courtyard. Concentric rows of villas oriented over the South China Sea follow this 30-acre (12.1-hectare) site's sloping contours, with its tropical gardens featuring thousands of trees. Among the hotel's 900-plus-piece art collection is a curving, large-scale Cor-Ten steel sculpture by the French artist Bernar Venet, which complements the property's architecture and topography.

All 112 accommodations received a refresh in 2021 by André Fu, who conceived the spaces as a dialogue with the original interior designer, the late Jaya Ibrahim. Fu kept the clean lines, adding sculptural lighting to soften the formality of these spaces. Fabricated in natural teak, oak, and rattan, Fu's bespoke furniture combines tropical elements with midcentury influences. These take inspiration from the abstract ink paintings of Wu Guanzhong and reflect the multifunctionality Fu prioritizes, evidenced in his low-slung sofa designed for lounging, working, and even sleeping, and a two-tiered table for dining and video calls. Known for his attention to detail, Fu's bedside lighting panel incorporates a ripple effect, reminiscent of the nearby beach. **—C.R.**

Halekulani Okinawa

Okinawa, Japan

Opened in 2019 as a sibling to the historic Halekulani hotel in Hawaii, the 360-room Halekulani Okinawa is situated on the western edge of Japan's southern island cluster, just north of Keramashoto National Park in the East China Sea. Complementing its tropical landscape, the property is dotted with swaying palm trees and the lilting vibe of life far closer to that of Oʻahu than Osaka. There's surfing, too, and perfect blue water, and the *Kariyushi* shirts that define the classic local outfit resemble the floral buttoned shirts synonymous with Hawaii.

The New York–based designer Alexandra Champalimaud brought her signature understated lushness to the interiors of this hotel, where the guest rooms' scheme is composed of seven subtly differentiated shades of white. The oversize rooms—each at least 538 square feet (50 square meters) or larger—are like cocoons, with white oak floors, custom rugs, and oblique nods to the locale, such as the grid pattern on each dresser that echoes a traditional Japanese shoji screen.

The minimalist interiors foreground the hotel's surroundings, sitting as it does in a national park; lush landscapes and a white-sand beach are just minutes' walk away. Then again, there's not necessarily a reason to set foot on the sand, since the 21-acre (8.5-hectare) site boasts five discrete pools, including the signature Orchid Pool, an outsize iteration of its eponym in Hawaii, with a giant cattleya orchid—the symbol of Halekulani—depicted in mosaic tiles on its floor. To anyone sauntering past at night, the lights make it glisten like a treasure.
—**M.E.**

Halekulani Okinawa

Imperial Hotel, Tokyo

Tokyo, Japan

Situated in Tokyo's Chiyoda-ku ward, just south of the Imperial Palace grounds and across the street from Hibiya Park, the Imperial Hotel, Tokyo, is both an architectural beacon and an oasis of hospitality in this bustling metropolis. First opened in 1890 as a Western-style guest house, the property has evolved over time to meet the culture around it. Most famously, the hotel was rebuilt in 1923 with a design by Frank Lloyd Wright. A reinforced-concrete structure crafted with golden brick and carved volcanic Oya stone, terra-cotta blocks, and hand-textured tiles, Wright's pyramid-like design was one of his most significant built in his lifetime, reflecting his deep engagement with Japanese culture. Following the 1964 Tokyo Olympics, plans were made for a new, modernized and expanded hotel by the architect Teitaro Takahashi, which opened in 1970 and resulted in the demolition of the Wright structure.

Today, the sprawling, 17-floor Imperial Hotel is home to 570 rooms, 27 banquet halls, a Shinto shrine, a tea-ceremony room, two wedding chapels, four bars, and 13 restaurants, including the Michelin-starred Les Saisons and the omakase-style Torakuro. Wonderfully, touches of Wright remain: Created in agreement with the Frank Lloyd Wright Foundation and completed in 2005, the 2,303-square-foot (214-square-meter) Frank Lloyd Wright Suite incorporates stained-glass windows and original carpets, furniture, and lighting, as well as special features inspired by his residential designs in the U.S. Guests can round out their stay with an expertly mixed cocktail at the Old Imperial Bar, where they can say *kampai* to a salvaged stone relief rescued from Wright's original masterpiece.
—**Spencer Bailey**

Lohkah Hotel & Spa

Xiamen, China

The 19th- and early-20th-century treaty port of Amoy—modern-day Xiamen—was an international city, a melting pot of cultures that influenced its food and architecture, seen to best effect in its trove of Chinese Art Deco homes. Overlooking Xiamen's marina, the Lohkah Hotel & Spa—the name is Sanskrit for "realm"—pays homage to that cosmopolitanism in its blend of contemporary and traditional. The regimented spaces, indoors and out, and the use of noble materials recall the rigor of Mies van der Rohe's Barcelona Pavilion, but the stone slab–clad complex, arranged in a loose, courtyard layout, can also be read as an angular interpretation of the circular *tulou* homes of Fujian's Hakka community.

Although it does convey order, this sleek minimalism is softened by earthy colors, warm lighting, and the generous use of wood. Also characteristic are the artful expanses of slender red brick used in Minnan architecture, an impressive 880,000 of which can be appreciated in Xia, one of two in-house restaurants, which serves a curated selection of fare traditional to Guangzhou and China's Fujian province.

There are 188 airy rooms, many of which overlook the South China Sea. Others gaze inward, on immaculately maintained gardens laid out by Indonesian architectural firm Intaran Design. An atmosphere of well-being pervades. One wing is dedicated to an outdoor Olympic pool and neutral-toned spa, where treatments nod to Xiamen's past, combining traditional Chinese medicine with Ayurveda in ways guaranteed to unkink the most knotted muscles. —**W.S.B.**

Lohkah Hotel & Spa

Lohkah Hotel & Spa

The Nai Harn

Phuket, Thailand

Even its competitors concede that The Nai Harn, Phuket's very first luxury resort, which opened in 1986, commands among the most idyllic locations on Thailand's best-known island. The hotel's white-concrete modernist structure cascades down a forested hillside on the rocky fringes of Nai Harn Beach, a secluded crescent sweep of sand lapped by incandescent waters. Renovations completed in 2016 by Bangkok's Habita Architects with new interiors by P49 Deesign harmonize the unquestionably 20th-century yet definitively timeless structure integrated into this niche of nearly untouched nature along Phuket's southern flank.

Public spaces highlighting the spectacular panorama fill a multistory plinth poised on the rocks, culminating in an open rooftop bar and sushi restaurant with cushioned loungers and cozy daybeds scattered around a reflecting infinity pool overlooking the Andaman Sea. Recessed into the hillside above, 120 light brown–washed wood and crisp white–lacquered guest rooms with natural rattan furniture and plush, checkerboard rugs evoke the feeling of a laidback beach house while focusing attention on the azure seascape. Plump, acid-green daybeds complete the sea-facing balconies, each hung with pink bougainvillea. The six mountain-facing rooms are equally serene, oriented toward the lush tropical vegetation outside.

Throughout, The Nai Harn's details are quintessentially Thai, from the painted-wood long-tail boats bobbing in the bay to the welcome bowls brimming with tropical delights such as pink dragon fruit and yellow mangoes. —**C.R.**

The Okura Tokyo

Tokyo, Japan

Text by **Spencer Bailey**
Photography by **Russel Wong**

Immediately upon entering The Okura Tokyo, located in the city's dense Toranomon business district, an "Okura aura" will wash over you. Step through the front door to the check-in desk of this vast, 508-room property, and an impressive choreography will ensue, swiftly transitioning you into an entirely different space of mind, body, and spirit. A world of Japanese simplicity, elegance, tradition, and innovation will seamlessly unfold. You may experience awe, or maybe even a floating feeling, as if you're in an ethereal dream. This hotel is so exquisite, so well-run, thought-through, and considered, that it seems almost too perfect for this world.

Since opening in 1962, The Okura's mission has been "best accommodation, best cuisine, best service," and it shows. To that, I would like to unofficially add: "best design." Though the original hotel, a midcentury icon designed by Yoshiro Taniguchi

Previous spread
An oversize flower arrangement inside the Prestige Tower's lobby, with beadlike lanterns hanging above.

Opposite, top to bottom
The Prestige Tower's lobby entrance lies just beyond the Okura Square's reflecting pool.

The lobby of The Okura Tokyo, as restored and resurrected to the original by the architect Yoshiro Taniguchi, located at the base of the Prestige Tower.

(1904–1979), was torn down—to some controversy and lamentation—in 2015, this clean slate made way for a sublimely sensitive overhaul and expansion: two new glass-curtained structures, the Prestige Tower and the adjacent Heritage Wing, opened in 2019 with interiors by Yoshiro's son, the renowned architect Yoshio Taniguchi, born in 1937 and best known for his redesign of New York's Museum of Modern Art.

Rich in history and representative of Japanese culture, this is a place that honors its lasting heritage at every turn. The lobby, first designed by Yoshiro, was painstakingly re-created and resurrected by Yoshio, who treated it with the utmost reverence and care, as something *hisei*, or sacred, passed from father to son. Extraordinarily, Yoshio not only faithfully reproduced the design, materials, and layout of his father's original creation (albeit turning the room 90 degrees), but also the atmosphere—the light, the acoustics, the temperature, the airflow, the feel. I visited the old Okura in early 2015, just before it was demolished, and as soon as I walked into the new lobby, I instantly sensed an uncanny familiarity. It was as if I'd been transported back in time to the old hotel—the space was much as I remembered it—only now, nestled within a 41-floor skyscraper, it felt refreshed and full of a new kind of energy.

There's an enduring intimacy to The Okura that belies the sleek high-rise it's located inside. Thankfully, the lobby remains the star of the show; without it, The Okura would not be *The Okura*. The oversize, expertly arranged flower vase; the beadlike lanterns strung together and delicately hung from the ceiling; the ornamental flower-petal textiles on the walls; the hemp-leaf *kumiko* lattices running along the windows; the bamboo shoji screens; the lacquered tables and chairs; and the classic world map sketch and Seiko wall clock—it's all still there, preserved, restored, and timelessly held in place.

The Prestige Tower itself is like a city within a city. Wedged—and practically hidden—between its eight-level base and upper floors are 18 floors of private offices. Starting on the 27th floor, there's a fitness center and spa with a five-lane, 82-foot (25-meter) pool, then guest rooms (floors 28–40) and a club lounge (floor 37), and on the very top, the Sazanka teppanyaki restaurant, the Starlight bar and lounge, and a "sky chapel" and banquet rooms. The lobby level includes the all-day-dining restaurant Orchid and the adjacent Orchid Bar, a jewelry boutique, and a flower shop, while the sixth floor houses the Toh-Ka-Lin Chinese restaurant, a "salon" space, and a business center with four private meeting rooms. More banquet rooms and a 15-store shopping arcade are also on site.

At the northwest corner of the Prestige Tower, a serene, portal-like hallway leads guests to the Heritage Wing, a 17-floor "annex" structure drenched in warm, clean-lined Japanese minimalism. Designed entirely by Yoshio and filled with *ikebana* arrangements and timeless décor, the building exudes a *tokonoma*-like sensibility. (For the uninitiated, a *tokonoma* is an alcove common in Japanese tearooms for displaying objects, pictures, and flowers.) A stairwell in the lobby—which includes a 41-foot (12.5-meter)-tall wisteria-shaped chandelier, conceived by the Beirut-born, Paris-based architect Lina Ghotmeh and made of purple-hued Czech glass—leads guests downstairs to the Japanese restaurant Yamazato, which

The Okura Tokyo

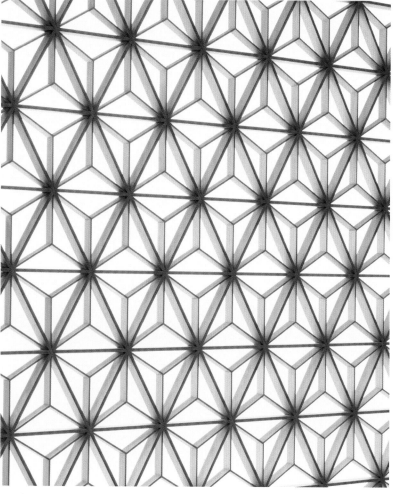

Opposite, clockwise from top
The lobby staircase in the Heritage Wing, with the Paris-based architect Lina Ghotmeh's "Wisteria Shadow" chandelier.

The entrance door to a lower-level banquet room, with brass door handles upcycled from the original Okura Tokyo.

A traditional *kumiko* lattice screen.

features the *sukiya*-style Chosho-an teahouse, originally built in 1962 by the master carpenter Sotoji Nakamura and sensitively installed by Yoshio. On the Heritage Wing lobby floor is a second restaurant, Nouvelle Epoque, which serves French cuisine. (Remarkably, Yamazato and Nouvelle Epoque are the only two restaurants in the world designed by Yoshio.) On the building's exterior, The Okura family crest, a *gokaibishi*, or five-layered diamond, runs up the walls, adding further texture to the building.

I stayed in one of the property's 140 spacious Heritage Rooms, which range from 570 to 678 square feet (53 to 63 square meters), and are just slightly larger in size than the Prestige Rooms housed in the neighboring tower. While decidedly contemporary in feeling, the meditative design of the Heritage Rooms evokes traditional Japanese architecture. Featuring grand views, the spaces summon a sense of *shakkei*, or "borrowed scenery," where the outside becomes a part of the inside. Then there are the high-end amenities: Each Heritage Room includes a steam room, as well as a jet bath, a heated bathroom floor, and a walk-in closet. Every night, immaculately ironed pajamas are laid out during turndown service. As a guest, it's impossible not to feel pampered.

The "gate" to this sprawling, shiny new campus is the enchanting Okura Square, which features a central 138-foot (42-meter)-wide water reflecting pool and a carpet-like road covered in granite and styled in *ichimatsu*, a classic Japanese checkered pattern. On the southwest corner of the site sits the Okura Museum of Art, originally designed by Itō Chūta and completed in 1927. Japan's oldest existing private art museum, it was founded by the businessman Kihachiro Okura, the father of the hotel's founder, Kishichiro Okura, and holds an impressive 2,500 works in its collection. Registered as a Tangible Cultural Property of Japan, the museum was moved 21 feet (6.5 meters) in order to accommodate the site's new layout, and its interior was subsequently renovated by Yoshio. In many ways, the museum and its holdings serve as a fitting, deep-rooted metaphor and framework for the entire Okura experience.

The refreshed site also includes a 3.2-acre (1.3-hectare) green space in the form of a garden. Inspired by the *kyokusui*, or "meandering water," garden previously located on the seventh floor of the original main building, this new space features hydrangeas, Siberian irises, and sweet flag grass; many replanted trees and replaced stones from the old structure; and even a camphor tree first planted by the Meiji-era admiral Tōgō Heihachirō.

Beyond The Okura's extraordinary design, it's the *omotenashi*, or supreme level of hospitality and mindfulness, that pervades the property. The service is so discreetly done that it practically dissolves (during my stay, there was always someone there to help, but never in a way that felt invasive). For Shinji Umehara, the president and representative director of The Okura Tokyo, the hotel serves as Japan's reception hall—something it has strived to be from the start. Located across the street from the U.S. embassy and the U.S. ambassador's residence, there is indeed a diplomatic—if decidedly low-key and unfussy—nature to the place. The Okura Tokyo invites you in with a graceful, elegant bow, and through both its highly refined design and sensitive service says, *"Irasshaimase."* Welcome.

This page
A private dining room in the restaurant Yamazato, located in the Heritage Wing.

Opposite
A section of the *Sanjuroku-nin Kashu*, or *"Thirty-Six Immortals of Poetry,"* panels in the Heritage Wing lobby, featuring paper from an old Okura banquet room.

Opposite
A lower-level foyer area, outside the banquet halls, with a wisteria trellis–inspired ceiling light fixture.

This page
Inside the "salon" space on the sixth floor of the Prestige Tower, overlooking Okura Square.

Asia, Australia & the Indian Ocean

The PuLi Hotel and Spa

Shanghai, China

Across Jing An Park from the golden temple of the same name, The PuLi Hotel and Spa lies behind delicate metal mesh screens and thatches of bamboo, its main entrance guarded by a phalanx of the stone lion posts once found outside wealthy Chinese homes. These decorative sculptures set the mood for the opulence within. The work of Australia's Layan Design Group—the force also behind The Setai, Miami Beach (page 78) and the Datai Langkawi in Malaysia—in association with the late Jaya Ibrahim, the interiors impress without being loud.

Antique touches, from delicate celadon vases to inkstone tabletops, exist harmoniously alongside contemporary Chinese art. Even basic elements, such as the dark, glossy flooring in the expansive lobby, come with a pedigree, produced by the former imperial factory in Beijing that still turns out replacement tiling, made of mud from the nearby Taihu Lake, for the Forbidden City.

The 229 rooms are pared down, in a cool contrast to the cultural treasures found elsewhere on the property. In-room seating, which ranges from sofas to separate lounge areas, is clearly designed to be used, not just appreciated for its form, and the metal mesh screens of the building's exterior reappear as curtains and room dividers, combining with the palette of off-whites and dark woods to create an atmosphere of intimacy and retreat—especially at night, when floor lamps spill pools of golden light. Place its vaulting dimensions aside, and The PuLi feels as much like the home of one of China's old aristocrat scholars as it does a sophisticated 21st-century hotel.
—**W.S.B.**

The PuXuan Hotel and Spa

Beijing, China

A thrilling addition to a burgeoning cultural cluster at the top of Beijing's tony Wangfujing Street, The PuXuan Hotel and Spa offers an exquisitely modern reinterpretation of the simple courtyard houses that once filled this neighborhood. Designed by German architect Ole Scheeren, the building is an enigma of porthole-pierced basalt topped by a honeycomb glass cube. From the use of natural materials to Chinese decorative inflections, it's clear that Shanghai-based interiors firm MQ Studio took the "Asian contemporary" brief to heart. The design is so beautifully done that the low-lit aesthetic and tactile surfaces have spawned a host of local lookalikes since the property opened, in 2019.

Hollow at its core, the hotel features 92 rooms and 24 suites across four floors, which are staggered so that the Zen water garden at the center is echoed in floating terraces. Right from the lobby, it's clear that art is a central concern, and while most is contemporary, and often breathtaking—take Qiu Deshu's monumental landscape *The Mountain*, for example—the classics also get a nod, largely in the form of ceramics.

Beijing may not be known for its quiet, but The PuXuan takes serenity seriously. Staff glide; doors shut softly; beds are sensibly separated from entranceways by sleek, ceiling-height partitions; and solid soundproofing turns the cityscape outside into a moving painting. The result feels like a series of nested jewel boxes with the guest as a prized possession. This hotel seduces with its location and design, but its tranquility is what leaves the most lasting impression.
—**W.S.B.**

The PuXuan Hotel and Spa

Signiel Seoul

Seoul, South Korea

Located atop Kohn Pedersen Fox's gleaming 1,821-foot (555-meter) Lotte World Tower—the sixth-tallest building in the world—Signiel Seoul holds the title of Korea's highest hotel. The compound is also home to an art museum, a concert hall, and an aquarium, and sits smack in the heart of Jamsil, a convenient hop from some of Seoul's best shopping and the serene Seokchon Lake Park. Spanning the 76th to 101st floors, the hotel is a declaration of intent by the country's fifth-largest *chaebol*, or family-owned business conglomerate, which has interests in retail, entertainment, travel, and hotels.

Wilson Associates' classical-meets-contemporary interiors are conceived of as "villas in the sky." Though delimited by the gentle curve of the tower, which narrows gracefully like the tip of an ink brush, little else about this airy flagship feels constrained—and that includes the heavenly views. The lighting, which varies from statement to subtle, is by Singapore's Project Lighting Design, whose judicious play on light and shade showcases the soaring, double-height ceilings and glossy surfaces in public areas via standout pieces, but in the 235 rooms, indirect lighting conjures up cocoons of comfort.

Fitted with Frette bedding and Vitra furniture, most of the rooms are finished in an eggshell palette of off-whites and gentle blues that echo the capital's skies, with *mugunghwa* floral motifs drawn from Korean ceramics. The bathrooms, which make the most of the aerial views, are finished in varying shades of marble, while the slight slope of the floor-to-ceiling windows in the elegantly appointed bedrooms adds a faintly nautical flair. —**W.S.B.**

Soori Bali

Bali, Indonesia

The prolific architect Soo K. Chan, known for his sculptural towers in urban centers ranging from New York to Kuala Lumpur, considers Soori Bali his most personal and intimate project. The Yale-trained, Singapore-based architect originally intended to construct his family's vacation home on this site along a black-sand beach in Bali's relatively untouched Tabanan Regency, but decided that the setting called for something more substantial. Overlooking the Indian Ocean and radiant green rice fields with sacred Mount Batukaru in the distance, it is an extraordinary enclave.

After preserving Bali's ancient *subak* irrigation system and the volcanic stone pathways to the property's nine Hindu shrines, Chan built a sleek sanctuary of 38 linear dwellings under double-height wooden rooftops, with structures made of gray *paras kelating* sandstone from a nearby quarry, *batu candi* lava stone that mirrors the black sand beach, and locally cast bronze. The low-lit spa features terra-cotta flower-patterned tiles crafted by artisans from nearby Pejaten.

Chan's holistic layout leverages traditional ecological knowledge, emphasizing the open courtyards and seamless transitions between indoors and out—a nod to his childhood home in Penang, Malaysia. Coconut palm, pandan, ipomea, and *pong-pong* trees surround ponds and reflection pools. Multiple windows in every interior space encourage north-south cross-ventilation and offer abundant sunlight, while overhanging roof eaves and ledges reduce reliance on air-conditioning. Naturally, since opening, in 2010, Soori Bali has consistently maintained the highest environmental standards.
—C.R.

Europe

Anantara The Marker Dublin Hotel

Dublin, Ireland

Opened in 2013 and rebranded by the Bangkok-based hotel group in 2023, Anantara The Marker Dublin Hotel is an unambiguously modern address with a historic moniker. Honoring the final iron indicator on the historic Grand Canal inland trade route connecting Dublin with mainland Europe, this property sits in the Docklands district, which in recent years has become an innovative technology hub.

Local firm MDO Architects took design cues from the hexagonal basalt stones of Northern Ireland's Giant's Causeway, a UNESCO World Heritage site, for the hotel's unusual checkerboard-glass façade. Conceiving the structure as a coastal form eroded over time, they approached the ground floor as a colossal cave, for which the structural engineering company Arup built a 220-foot (67-meter) bridge with no intermediate supports. Here, the abstractly patterned carpeting calls to mind the stratus clouds that often blanket Irish skies.

The cantilevered block above holds 187 rooms and suites. Floor-to-ceiling windows facing both the city and the Wicklow Mountains bring natural light into these spaces for which Irish designers crafted the ergonomic furniture in soft, autumnal-hued fabrics, accentuating the vibrancy of the deep-purple carpeting. In the low-lit spa, dark walnut floor panels and stone walls set off the electric-orange loungers, the celadon-green ceiling, and the beryl blue-tiled, 75-foot (23-meter)-long swimming pool. Upstairs on the seventh floor, in the rooftop bar's jagged cocktail tables and low-slung modular couches inspired by the Burren, a wild, rocky landscape in the country's southwest region, the designers leaned into Ireland's landscape once more. **—C.R.**

Avant Mar

Paros, Greece

Parian marble, named for its origins on the Cycladic island of Paros, was used to sculpt such Greek masterpieces as *Venus de Milo* and *Winged Victory of Samothrace*. This milky-white metamorphic rock also aptly features in the design of Avant Mar—literally "in front of the sea"—which opened on Paros's crown-jewel Piperi Beach in 2023.

Designed by the Athens-based Tense Architecture Network, the resort makes a bold first impression with its circular reception building and elliptical wellness area, the latter inspired by the fourth-century thermal baths at the Sanctuary of Asclepius at Epidaurus, dedicated to the god of medicine and healing, on the Greek mainland. Mirroring surrounding Cycladic fishing villages, stacked white sugar cube-like structures climb the hillside, housing 38 rooms, including eight suites with private pools. Marble features prominently in these Chadios Architects-designed sanctuaries, most notably in the asymmetrical white-marble slab flooring—a modern version of traditional Cycladic paving—and in the bathrooms' black-veined white-marble countertops. It's not all ancient Greek here, though: An oversize room mirror conceals a television, and a built-in Bluetooth sound system connects to ceiling speakers. Many rooms overlook the 180-foot (55-meter)-long swimming pool that runs through the property toward the Aegean Sea.

Curved arches, recessed niches, and geometric patterns—design elements updated from traditional Parian architecture—are complemented by blues and whites throughout the public areas. A modern Japanese aesthetic blends seamlessly with this Cycladic style at the Matsuhisa Paros restaurant, a Nobu outpost especially memorable for its gentle curves and wooden cylindrical frames set within a Mediterranean garden by the sea. —**C.R.**

Bairro Alto Hotel

Lisbon, Portugal

Located in Lisbon's historic Luís de Camões Square, the Bairro Alto Hotel first opened in 2005 and was updated in 2019 by the Porto-based architect Eduardo Souto de Moura. The Pritzker Prize winner's design brings together the hotel's mid-18th-century foundation with three adjacent Pombaline-era structures, preserving the original masonry, vaults, and tiles, and their Easter-egg shades of buttermilk, seafoam, and pistachio.

Porto interiors firm Atelier Bastir added its expertise in home design to the 87 guest rooms, filling each with Portuguese crafts-manship, from artisanal rugs and rattan-embellished cabinets to hand-painted bird frescoes and Barro tiles to playful Anna Westerlund ceramics in the suites. The communal areas feel homey, too, with vintage furniture collected in Paris, Brussels, and Milan, as well as contemporary art by José Pedro Cortes, Pedro Cabrita Reis, and Rui Chafes. A polychromatic macramé tapestry by Diana Meneses Cunha, of Oficina 166, extends over three floors, depicting the city's seven hills.

The four dining options are helmed by the celebrated Portuguese chef Nuno Mendes. Clad in polished wood, with the rounded edges typical of traditional Lisbon pâtisseries, Pastelaria serves nontraditional dishes, such as wine and garlic chicken pies and Madeiran banana bread, all made with Portuguese organic flour. At the fifth-floor BAHR & Terrace restaurant, designed by Thestudio, curved walls and an elongated oval window overlooking the Tagus River channel vintage ships, while the open kitchen, with its vast marble countertop, puts dishes influenced by bygone trade routes and prod-ucts brought from distant lands on full display. **—C.R.**

Bayerischer Hof

Munich, Germany

In the heart of Munich's tidy, largely uniform historic district lies Bayerischer Hof, whose verdant rooftop terrace cascades dramatically down above the hotel's Bavarian blue awnings. The 337-room hotel's design unfurls as a palimpsest across eight floors shared between its main body and its annex. From its ballroom and cinema to its event spaces and jazz club, the interior shape-shifts between stately and svelte, an effect achieved through a series of streamlined renovations and additions. For nearly two centuries, the hotel—a stay of choice for locals and visiting royals alike—has harmonized traditional and modern aesthetics to transcend typical conceptions of luxury.

For a taste of the hotel as it was in eras past, grab an aperitif in Falk's Bar, a mirrored 19th-century room, before dinner at the two-Michelin-starred restaurant Atelier. The intimate dining establishment is a paradigm of the multi-hyphenate Belgian designer Axel Vervoordt's influence on the hotel: His penchant for understated beauty also inspired dozens of the rooms and suites, including the crowning Penthouse Garden Suite. Rough-hewn woods and lime mortar pigments in each Vervoordt-designed space offer a neutral palette upon which sunlight—cast through floor-to-ceiling windows—paints a glowing finish.

On the upper floors, guests can take respite at the Blue Spa, designed by the late French interiors doyenne Andrée Putman, which features a pool with a sliding-glass roof, or at the modernist bar and lounge designed by Sanjit Manku of the Paris-based firm Jouin Manku. Topped by a solarium deck, the hotel ensures year-round access to views of the city—vantage points that have been enjoyed here for generations.
—Hazen Mayo

Bayerischer Hof

Bill&Coo Mykonos

Mykonos, Greece

Set across two coastal locales on Mykonos (with villas on a third site), both overlooking the dazzling aquamarine waters of the Aegean Sea, Bill&Coo Mykonos is an ode to its paradisiacal surroundings. Behind Cycladic-inspired façades both minimalist and organic, an earthy interior palette pervades through soft white walls, bleached wood, and local stone, cultivating a meditative feel throughout.

In the Megali Ammos location—a mere 10-minute stroll from Mykonos Town—32 sea-view suites designed by K-Studio and three bamboo-roofed villas by Divercity Architects dapple the coastal hillside, while an infinity pool with starlike lighting comes to life as the sun sets. Those seeking a more serene and intimate setting can venture to the far-west region of Agios Ioannis, where the hotel's Coast Suites, a cluster of bungalows, are tucked into a secluded cove. Polished screed and marble floors, wooden trellises, and bespoke chestnut furniture bestow a tranquil, monastic quality on the original 15 suites here, while expansive terraces with private pools at the 10 newer suites, designed by People Architects, afford an added level of privacy. White stone and verdant rushes implemented by landscape architects Greenways demarcate spaces while preserving breathtaking views of the sea, the nearby chapel of St. John, and Delos Island in the distance.

After a day of poking into local artisan shops, snorkeling at Paradise Reef, or simply soaking up sun, guests can bask in a leisurely alfresco meal at Beefbar Mykonos, where the street food menu is split into three categories: "Leaf," "Beef," and "Reef." —**E.J.**

Botanic Sanctuary Antwerp

Antwerp, Belgium

Text by **Cynthia Rosenfeld**
Photography by **Frederik Vercruysse**

What do you get when you combine a former intensive-care nurse, a trained architect turned real estate developer, a medieval hospital, and one of Europe's most design-driven cities?

The answer—Botanic Sanctuary Antwerp— is a true urban oasis set alongside municipal gardens at the edge of the city's historic center, gracefully assembled from stylistically disparate structures of various periods, on grounds with a tradition of caregiving dating back eight centuries. Opened in 2022, this 108-room hotel—the vision of local developer Eric De Vocht and his wife, Maryse Odeurs, the aforementioned nurse—includes six restaurants (already awarded four Michelin stars among them), two bars and a by-invitation whiskey cellar, a spa with 10 treatment rooms, an apothecary, a historic chapel, a theater, 18 conference rooms, and three organic gardens. The couple set out to celebrate

Antwerp, a city historically known as the capital of the world's diamond trade, by creating a sophisticated platform to show off its best—from the trove of Flemish Old Master works at the Royal Museum of Fine Arts Antwerp to up-and-coming jewelry designers such as Elliott & Ostrich—while making everyone feel welcome.

Odeurs stressed their vision of hospitality to me when she and I walked the five-acre (two-hectare), leaf-covered grounds on a cool autumn morning; it's also something I observed firsthand throughout my stay. Whether guests come for traditional afternoon pancakes at the "Hansel and Gretel"–like, Michelin-starred restaurant Het Gebaar; post up for a night in an entry-category, 269-square-foot (25-square-meter) Classic Room; or opt for an extended stay in the 1,507-square-foot (140-square-meter) Botanic Suite, this genuine sense of welcome pervades the property. To help achieve it, the couple made the decision to eschew handing over management to a luxury hotel operator, ardently believing that remaining independent would be key to their project's success.

De Vocht and Odeurs's passion—and resources—fueled extensive negotiations with the city, which owns the land (their IRET Development firm holds a 66-year lease, with discussions underway to extend it to 90 years), followed by four years of painstaking restoration, construction, and interior design. De Vocht had long admired the motley complex of historic buildings and gardens located between Lange Gasthuisstraat Sint-Jorispoort and Leopoldstraat, where nine Gothic arches mark the entrance, in Antwerp's historic Theaterbuurt, or "Theater Area," so-called for its proximity to both the French and Flemish opera houses.

Antwerp's oldest document, dated 1226, granted permission for the first *hospitale infirmorum* to be erected in the vicinity of what is now the deconsecrated Cathedral of Our Lady, served by laypeople who later adopted the monastic rule of Saint Augustine. A larger hospital, named after Saint Elisabeth of Hungary, opened in 1238. Though nothing remains of these original hospices, tales of the institute's nuns and monks growing vegetables and herbs for food and remedies while caring for its inhabitants laid the groundwork for this ambitious 21st-century undertaking. Today, the oldest buildings on the hotel's grounds are the Romanesque-style chapel, erected around 1400 (and extended between 1442–1460), and the Gothic infirmary— Europe's oldest—dating to 1460. In the 16th century, the respected apothecary Pieter Coudenberg established a medicinal herb garden adjacent to the hospital, the precursor of the city's present-day Botanical Garden. After the religious institution was dissolved, in 1797, the hospital was placed under the administration of the predecessor to the current Public Center for Social Welfare, which enlarged and remodeled the compound over the ensuing centuries, until 2017, when De Vocht and Odeurs stepped in to restore the buildings and reinvent the site.

Sitting down under a Matteo Pugliese bronze male nude at the cozy Henry's Bar, AIDarchitecten co-founder Kristl Bakermans Le Bon made it clear that she and her partner, Gerd van Zundert, had much to unravel in the summer of 2017, when their Antwerp-based architecture firm was hired to figure out what to do with the assortment of historic buildings and drab modern additions. Stripped of these superfluities and ad hoc patching, the original

stonework and structures emerged, as did the site's beauty and potential. The architects gained clarity that this project—which would ultimately comprise some 215,278 square feet (20,000 square meters) of built space—should evolve as a succession of spaces distinct in their identity, dimensions, and appearance.

Over four years, five architects worked on the site full time, occasionally even digging up the ground with spoons alongside archeologists. They adapted historic building techniques and repurposed materials including wood—some of it 400 years old—and stone, as well as original door hinges. Buildings were restored wherever possible while respecting their original functions: Two former monastery kitchens became the private dining rooms Culina Romana and Culinary Batavica, their walls clad entirely in 18th-century blue-and-white Delft tiles commonly gifted among nuns, while the monastery's 19th-century pharmacy serves as a botanical apothecary.

For every newly built element, the architects opted for a wholly contemporary design, even while prioritizing historical craftsmanship, employing natural materials such as Pierre Bleu stone quarried in the south of Belgium and lime and chalk to plaster the walls. Local builders and craftspeople deftly connected the new and protected architectural entities, often by elegant glass conservatory constructions based on the winter garden canopy of the grounds' original 19th-century guesthouse.

One of these airy conservatories became Henry's Bistro, where vines climb the monastery's original brick façade and dishes unite Belgian ingredients with international cuisine. In the cavernous Catalpa breakfast room, with its historic wood-beam ceiling and wide-plank floors, guests can start their mornings with chewy pretzel bread and *neteling*, an herb goat cheese variety from the noted Belgian cheesemakers Fréderic and Michel Van Tricht. Then there's the celebrated Amsterdam-based chef Jacob Jan Boerma's Fine Fleur, where the local architect Dennis T'Jampens chose subtle down and up spotlights, oak beam and bronze mirror ceilings, and raw limed walls to accentuate the room's time-worn roughness, juxtaposed against large, smooth blocks of kaleidoscopic Belvedere granite slabs.

Another of the hotel's restaurants—open only 10 days each month—is the West Flemish garden-driven Hertog Jan, which shocked Belgian gastronomes by closing its three-Michelin-starred Zedelgem flagship near Bruges in 2018. Interior architect and designer Benoit Viaene created the soothing, organic design of this former cloister space with neutral clay walls, oak wood floors, cork stools, and just seven refreshingly tactile, handcrafted dark wood tables placed at a thoughtful distance from one another and set with only the essentials, including smooth, flat-as-a-pancake stone placemats. Without giving away too much of the surprise awaiting fortunate future diners, Viaene built a curvilinear dining cocoon facing chef Gert de Mangeleer's emerald-tiled kitchen, unseen upon arrival and inspired by the local tradition of dining at the kitchen table, with dishes served on twee Royal Boch porcelain that many Belgians will remember from their grandparents' homes. Ingredients for this revered three-hour omakase meal include flowers, herbs, and tomatoes from the hotel's greenhouse and garden.

Opposite
Culinary Batavica, one of the hotel's two old monastery kitchens, its walls clad in 18th-century blue-and-white Delft tiles.

This page
The stairwell seen from the ground floor of the Hospitum building.

Botanic Sanctuary Antwerp

That olfactory oasis of chamomile, sage, valerian, rosemary, basil, juniper, and mint also serves the adjacent 10,764-square-foot (1,000-square-meter) Botanic Health Spa, whose emphasis is on healing plants and herbs. Compelled by her fervent belief in preventative medicine, Odeurs hired the spa's osteopath, Xavier Le Clef, to develop technology-driven treatments that detect underlying conditions and help prevent disease rather than merely kneading aches and pains. Design-wise, the spa's centerpiece is the 59-foot (18-meter)-long swimming pool, encased in a glass shed overlooking the garden on one side and historic Flemish façades on the other. It's an especially ravishing scene after dark, when the pool's stainless-steel lining turns the water a mesmerizing electric blue.

Odeurs took equal interest in the hotel rooms, determined to fill them with what the two love in their home outside Antwerp—warm earthy colors, tactile textures, modern art including works by Jean Cocteau, and antiques collected during their travels to Asia and Africa. Along with creating a separate mood board for each individual room and suite, interior designer Rebecca Verstraete also had access to the owners' warehouse full of antiques. She describes this project as more akin to furnishing a house than a hotel. Natural stone, plaster walls, and Belgian linens unify the accommodations, spread across five heritage buildings—Sint-Joris; Sint-Elisabeth; Alnetum; Filips van Marnixhuis; and the oldest, Monasterium. Formerly home to pastors and nuns, the historic structure now houses terraced suites overlooking the chapel as well as rooms directly under the pitched ceiling entirely lined in centuries-old wood beams.

To walk around Botanic Sanctuary with these three accomplished women—the designer, the architect, and the co-owner—was to appreciate the magnificence of its reinvention. Both Verstraete and Bakermans Le Bon compare the project to the slow, methodical progress of fitting together pieces of a puzzle. Most of all, they credit Odeurs for her consistent eye and commitment to hospitality and care, and De Vocht, true to his architecture training, for always opting for quality and long-term solutions. In every aspect of this Edenic refuge, the couple's devotion is evident.

Capri Tiberio Palace

Capri, Italy

Capri Tiberio Palace could be considered the cheeky, subversive younger sibling of the stuffier hotels that have long had a stranglehold on high-end hospitality in Capri. The interiors, from Milan-based Giampiero Panepinto, are shot through with wit and color in equal doses. A maximalist triumph, every surface is considered, from the walls, where bright stripes jostle for attention with framed monochrome snapshots of 1960s starlets, to the shelves and tables, which are festooned with curios such as a miniature Riva speedboat and a pile of art books including a *Playboy* anthology or two. Sniff the air to catch a whiff of Fiori di Capri, a scent made by the local perfumer Carthusia and based on a formula dating back almost centuries.

None of the 54 rooms and suites are alike, though almost all of them have a balcony or terrace about the same size as the room itself, decorated in handmade majolica tiling. Guests can order a cocktail or two at Jacky Bar—where one wall is decorated entirely with Borsalino hats and where a crooner-ready white grand piano stands at ease in the corner— then spend the next morning poolside or at the on-site restaurant before venturing out once the day-trippers have departed; the Capri Tiberio Palace is handily sequestered from the hubbub of the *piazzetta*, but only a short walk away. To cap the day, an aperitif at Terrazza Tiberio on the ground floor hits the spot—the sofa at the rear being the best place to see locals out for their evening walk, or *passeggiata*. —**M.E.**

Capri Tiberio Palace

Casa Angelina

Praiano, Italy

Perched atop the Amalfi Coast cliffs in the sleepy fishing village of Praiano—a blissful respite from the tourist-filled buzz of nearby Positano and Capri—and with just 37 keys, Casa Angelina lives up to the quaint, homey feel of its name. Conceived by local architect Gennaro Fusco in 2005 as one of the first contemporary properties on this pristine Mediterranean coastline, the hotel is open seasonally from April through October.

Behind the seamless white-on-white scheme is local designer Marco de Luca, whose minimalist, subtly modern taste pervades throughout. In the lounge spaces, canvas-like walls and neutral-colored sofas and armchairs serve as the backdrop for vivid abstract oil paintings by Patricia Valencia Carstens, Murano glass sculptures by Alfredo Sosabravo, surrealist furniture from Gervasoni, and pleated lamps designed by Philippe Starck for Flos. Breezy curtains frame postcard-worthy views of the Tyrrhenian Sea. The Azure Suite features shades of blue carefully selected by Paola Lenti to echo the sea and sky, and is filled out with her designs, including gloss-varnished Strap side tables, a Silent bed, and an Agio chaise longue. Balconies or wide terraces in all the rooms and a central glass elevator ensure that guests don't miss a moment of the surrounding vistas.

Outside, a sun-drenched pool deck spreads out beside a lemon tree–adorned pergola, such that a soft breeze brings with it traces of citrus and sea. From there, guests can take in the panorama of nearby brightly hued houses, craggy cliffs, and—on a cloudless day—the sculptural Faraglioni rocks that dot the coast of Capri. **—E.J.**

Casa Baglioni Milan

Milan, Italy

Nestled in the heart of the Brera design district, Casa Baglioni Milan pays tribute to Italy's 1960s heyday. Inside the 1913 Art Nouveau building, a flamboyant zigzag carpet references the architecture and design of Gio Ponti, whose canary-yellow velvet sofa inhabits the lobby, a rotating art gallery dedicated to Italian masters and up-and-coming international artists. Hanging above is a neon chandelier by the Italian light-maker Panzeri, which channels Lucio Fontana's light sculpture in the nearby Museo del Novecento. The hotel's Gio Ponti walking tour emblematizes its mission to celebrate native artisanship, from everyday objects to city landmarks.

Local interior design studio Spagnulo & Partners filled the hotel's interiors with custom wallpaper and furnishings by Rubelli, textural fabrics by Dedar, and bathroom fittings by Zucchetti Kos. The common areas, including the wine cellar and the Michelin-starred restaurant helmed by chef Claudio Sadler, integrate handmade vases, trays, and plates that mix clear and colored glass with metal and ceramics by Gala Rotelli. On the rooftop, lounge chairs, sofas, and stainless-steel side tables by Paola Lenti are set on her modular rugs woven with Twitape yarn.

Among the many works in the hotel's art collection are *Bianco* (1973), by Agostino Bonalumi, and Enrico Castellani's *Superficie Bianca* (2003), both in the lobby, as well as Carla Accardi's *Assedio Rosso* (1955), Christo and Jeanne-Claude's *Running Fence* (1974), and multiple 1960s Hans Hartung pieces. In the 30 rooms and suites, meticulous Italian craftsmanship extends to the bathrooms, which feature bold herringbone wood panels that climb the shower walls.
—C.R.

Casa Baglioni Milan

The Chedi Andermatt

Andermatt, Switzerland

Nestled at the crossroads of Switzerland's Oberalp, St. Gotthard, and Furka mountain passes, the village of Andermatt, with its dark wood chalets beneath snow-capped peaks, was best known for the 1964 James Bond film *Goldfinger*—until 2013, when Jean-Michel Gathy of the Kuala Lumpur-based architecture firm Denniston completed The Chedi Andermatt. With their astonishing proportions, its four commanding structures and their exposed wooden beams under gabled roofs reflect the Alpine town and its stunning surroundings.

Beneath a double-height, recessed ceiling is the ski lodge's capacious lobby, comprising black lacquered columns with fireplaces ringed by indulgently oversize divans and topped with faux-fur pillows and throws. Spin Studio's Yasuhiro Koichi designed the hotel's restaurant, which features wraparound floor-to-ceiling windows, lattice wood screens, and a 16-foot (4.9 meter)-tall walk-in cheese cellar. Further escalating the awe are the two-Michelin-starred dining destinations housed inside architect Christina Seilern's modern timber-and-stone cabin wedged onto Mount Gütsch at 7,546 feet (2,300 meters) above sea level. Accessible by gondola, the Japanese at Gütsch pays homage to the august setting in wood and stone.

A Swiss-chocolate palette pervades the property's 117 cozy, wood-paneled guest rooms and suites, each furnished with supple leather couches, club chairs, and a dual-sided fireplace, visible from the marble bathroom's cavernous soaking tub. —**C.R.**

The Dolder Grand

Zurich, Switzerland

City and country coalesce at The Dolder Grand, a hilltop escape on the outskirts of Zurich that boasts views of Lake Zurich and the Alps. Originally opened in 1899, the palatial, château-style hotel was reimagined by Foster + Partners between 2004 and 2008. The result is a faithfully restored main building that preserves its majestic façade, topped with its original copper turrets and now flanked by two contemporary curvilinear wings wrapped with stencil-cut aluminum screens, their tree pattern reflecting the surrounding forests.

The 175 rooms and suites are set across both the main building and modern wings, many of them with private terraces and floor-to-ceiling curved windows. The arts pervade both public and private spaces here, with the Presidential Suites reflective of notable past guests, such as the Austrian conductor Herbert von Karajan, the sculptor Alberto Giacometti, and the Rolling Stones. The hotel's art collection features some 120 works by Swiss artists such as Urs Fischer and Max Bill, as well as international luminaries, living and dead, including Salvador Dalí, Joan Miró, Henry Moore, and Anselm Kiefer.

Among the seven dining options here are The Restaurant, which boasts two Michelin stars and is overseen by chef Heiko Nieder; The Saltz, designed by artist Rolf Sachs; and Mikuriya, a sleek omakase experience. The 43,056-square-foot (4,000-square-meter) spa is yet another major draw, with its winding pale stone walls perforated to allow in natural light, indoor and outdoor pools, 20 treatment rooms, fitness studio, plunge pools, and solarium. Geothermal heat pumps beneath the building contribute to a sustainability strategy pursued by Foster + Partners for the renovations that doubled floor space while halving energy consumption.
—C.O.E.

The Dylan Amsterdam

Amsterdam, The Netherlands

Among the canal houses of Keizersgracht in Amsterdam's Negen Straatjes ("Nine Streets") quarter, a 17th-century stone archway marks the entrance to The Dylan Amsterdam, a contemporary hotel rich with history. Originally Amsterdam's first theater, where Rembrandt worked and Vivaldi later served as orchestra conductor, it became a Catholic orphanage, then an almshouse, and in 1999, an Anouska Hempel–designed hotel, later renovated and reopened as The Dylan Amsterdam in 2004. Only the gate, spared during a 1772 fire, has remained throughout.

The charcoal façade gives way to the calming interiors of the Netherlands-based Studio Linse, designers of the nearby Rijksmuseum and London's Royal Opera House. In Bar Brasserie Occo, the firm lacquered the original terra-cotta tiles to a high gloss, adding oversize blue-gray leather sofas, marble tables, and a 16-foot (4.9-meter) brass chandelier over the solid marble bar. A single arch swathed in velvet leads into Restaurant Vinkeles, where the medieval ovens and bricks of a converted 18th-century bakery now decorate this modern take on classic French fare.

Housed between four 17th-century buildings and one building from 1902, 41 rooms conjure four distinct themes. Loxura rooms, designed by FG Stijl, are awash in opulent coppers, with bronze mirrors and mother-of-pearl details; Amber rooms get filled with earthy greens. Especially contemporary are the Serendipity rooms, featuring wenge floors, gray-and-coffee furnishings, and leather accents. Guests willing to climb a few steps are rewarded with the high drama of the top floor Lofts, with their bright white walls and exposed beams, finished with custom-made quartzite vanities and oakwood cabinets. —C.R.

Falkensteiner Hotel Kronplatz

Riscone di Brunico, Italy

The dramatic peaks of the Dolomites serve as a constant muse to the people of South Tyrol, an Italian region along the Austrian border known for its natural splendor and immeasurable bounty. This relationship is central to every element of the 97-room Falkensteiner Hotel Kronplatz, which is nestled at the base of the eponymous ski resort and at the entrance to the mountainous UNESCO World Heritage property.

Architect and designer Matteo Thun carefully tucked the Falkensteiner into the valley's foothills, abiding their gentle lull. Atop the knoll, four wood buildings interpret a regional vernacular with contemporary timber-and-glass framing. Kronplatz's intrinsic beauty spills into the hotel's foyer via tall wheatgrass and an impressive maple tree. A tiered garden of neat geometric plots sits at the axis of the campus, and rustic wood paneling blankets the gathering spaces and rooms.

The Falkensteiner immerses guests in Alpine-Mediterranean life and its passionate traditions of both outdoor sport and holistic wellness. Spanning 15,070 square feet (1,400 square meters), the Acquapure Summit Spa is equipped with a rooftop pool and sunbathing terrace, while the hotel's suites boast heated balconies and, in the case of the Summit Suites, Finnish saunas. Experienced concierges guide guests through a variety of skiing, hiking, climbing, and biking expeditions, from traversing beloved trails to off-piste exhilaration. Back on the property, the hotel's numerous relaxation rooms await, ready to rejuvenate the weary—as does the reception area, replete with homey parlors, fireplaces, and supple Italian loungers. Centered around a decorative tree and with a bar toward the back, it's an ideal place to decompress and socialize. —H.M.

Falkensteiner Hotel Kronplatz

Falkensteiner Hotel Montafon

Tschagguns, Austria

A family-friendly refuge in the Austrian forests of Montafon Valley, the Falkensteiner Hotel Montafon inhabits a duo of elongated structures whose punctuated façades practically reach out to touch the landscape. Wrapping the entire complex, which opened in 2022, is an eye-catching continuum of vertical wood slats that honors the region's architectural vernacular. Overall, the building's design, by the Oslo- and New York–based firm Snøhetta, focuses on children and families as its primary users, incorporating age-specific facilities such as a science lab, a multisport hall, a media room, and an indoor climbing wall, and integrating outdoor activity areas into the design's topography.

Renowned for its innovative, atypical structures such as the Oslo Opera House, Snøhetta nested the Falkensteiner's communal areas—the lobby, bar, restaurant, and spa—at the base of the mountain slope, merging the property with the rugged terrain. For the interiors, Milan- and Shanghai-based Vudafieri Saverino Partners looked to the immediate surroundings at various times of year to create the main color schemes, manifesting as a bright meadow-green and a blue referencing the nearby Ill River. Stacked above, in two interconnected three-story rectangular blocks, each of the 123 guest rooms delivers unobstructed alpine panoramas, many with single and bunk beds for traveling families. Vudafieri Saverino selected warm autumnal shades for these interiors: burnt orange for the carpets, scarlet red for the window drapes, and flaxen yellow for the couches.

Situated within Austria's first climate-neutral ski resort, the adventure mountain Golm, the hotel achieves net-zero emissions through CO_2 compensation, serving alpine-sourced cuisine, and operating its own biomass heating system. —**C.R.**

The Fontenay

Hamburg, Germany

Amid classic, rectilinear buildings dating back to Germany's Wilhelmine period (1890–1918), this curvaceous work of architecture fits contextually within Hamburg's Rotherbaum neighborhood, owing in part to the 1953 Alster Ordinance, which decreed that all façades be painted white. For The Fontenay, which opened in 2018 on the western shore of Alster Lake, a place of unexpected tranquility in the city center, local architect Jan Störmer evolved his amorphous design from three intertwining circles.

At the entrance, *Heaven Mirror*, a 45-foot (13.7 meter)-wide circular mosaic made from more than 200 granite blocks, reflects the sky and the surrounding 130-year-old plane trees. The seven-story building narrows in the pear-shaped central atrium, which is flooded with natural light reflected from 198 mirrored glass panels fitted with individually controlled, multiphase motors. Hanging within the 88-foot (27-meter)-high space is a dazzling 20-foot (6.1-meter) light sculpture by Brand van Egmond. Upstairs at the sixth-floor Fontenay Bar, dark herringbone parquet floors made from steamed spruce meet walls clad in Makassar ebony.

The building's singular shape compelled interior designer Christian Meinert of the Berlin-based firm Aukett + Heese to customize nearly every element in the 130 trapezoid-shaped guest rooms, down to the oak wood parquet flooring, sourced from the forest of the Fontenay Abbey in Burgundy, France. The hotel's intentional design ensured that all balconies face outward toward the lake or to the greenery of the surrounding neighborhood. The rooms feature specially woven Tai Ping rugs; objets from the Danish design house Georg Jensen; and artworks by the Peruvian painter Antonio Maro and the surrealist German photographer Jaschi Klein. —C.R.

The Fontenay

Gran Hotel Inglés

Madrid, Spain

When it opened in 1886, Gran Hotel Inglés received wide praise in Spanish newspapers for having an elevator, bathrooms on each floor, and electric lighting. Nearly a century and a half later, husband-and-wife hoteliers Carmen Cordón Muro and Ignacio Jiménez Artacho turned the page on this storied address in the city's historic Barrio de las Letras quarter, hiring the New York- and Madrid-based firm Rockwell Group, renowned for designing everything from Broadway musical sets to world-class restaurants, to undertake a comprehensive renovation. Staying faithful to local architect Juan José Sánchez Pescador's original design, Rockwell also firmly evolved the property—Madrid's first-ever hotel—into the 21st century.

Rockwell mined the hotel's rich history, mounting time-faded photographs of celebrated former hotel guests and hanging salvaged chandeliers between restored wooden columns. Balancing out these relics are sophisticated, modern shades of burnt orange, silver, ochre, and teal. The lobby's 20-foot (six-meter)-high ceilings reinforce the grandeur of this vast space, which is anchored by a circular central bar and warmed by clusters of cozy sitting areas with round-edged, caramel leather sofas and high-back armchairs on plush bespoke rugs. Nearby, the ground floor library is stocked with more than 600 books and features a wood-burning fireplace.

Upstairs, in the 48 spacious guest rooms and suites, Rockwell's Broadway background manifests in white wall moldings extending dramatically down from the ceiling, bronze Art Deco–inspired chandeliers, and closets wallpapered with images of vintage hotel postcards. Hardwood floors, walls lined with padded leather panels, and furnishings and fabrics designed by Rockwell round out these sophisticated sanctuaries. —C.R.

Grand Hotel Principe di Piemonte

Viareggio, Italy

When Grand Hotel Principe di Piemonte, a five-story Art Nouveau extravaganza on the waterfront in Viareggio, opened in 1922, its exuberant, balconied façade made it an instant landmark. The property became a magnet for the glitterati idling on the Tuscan riviera, from Marlene Dietrich to Sophia Loren to the Duke and Duchess of Windsor. It retains that cachet today, though the visiting crowd has pivoted to the world's super-rich; it's in Viareggio, after all, that most of the superyacht builders have their headquarters, a short walk from the seafront site of this 80-room hotel.

One hundred years after opening, the structure underwent a major renovation masterminded by S+S studio, a Florence-based team that—with the help of craftsmen living and working in Tuscany—restored all of its carved fixtures while adding fresh flourishes, heavy on brushed brass and wood, to every room. It fell to Florentine menswear designer Stefano Ricci to reimagine the 1,507-square-foot (140-square-meter), two-bedroom Presidential Suite. Stepping inside is like walking into a jewel box, with quilted leather and stained-glass accents glinting off the high-gloss surfaces.

The hotel's restaurant, Il Piccolo Principe, helmed by the chef Giuseppe Mancino, boasts two Michelin stars and is open for dinner Tuesdays through Saturdays and for lunch on Sundays. At the hotel breakfast, served in the elegant Tapestry Room, guests can try one of the à la carte egg dishes, each of which uses locally sourced eggs from a nearby farm, where the proprietor rears a range of rare breeds. —**M.E.**

Grand Park Hotel Rovinj

Rovinj, Croatia

Where the pine tree–covered hills of Monte Mulini meet the Mediterranean Sea in Rovinj, on the west coast of Croatia's Istria Peninsula, sits the Grand Park Hotel Rovinj. Here, starting from the hotel's main entrance—on the sixth and highest floor, where its three outdoor pools are—Zagreb-based Studio 3LHD designed a glass-and-steel structure that cascades down the terrain's natural slope, optimizing its beguiling waterfront vistas of Katarina Island. Deep roof canopies planted with indigenous vegetation shade lower floors that extend to generous garden terraces, swimming pools, and sundecks. This emphasis on landscaping continues down to the five-century-old Aleppo pines that stand where the hotel connects to a walking promenade.

Milan-based architect and designer Piero Lissoni cites Rovinj's sea-scape and forested environs as his primary inspirations for the hotel's interior, evident in the indigo blues and white, along with shades of burgundy, orange, gray, and khaki, seen throughout. Lissoni & Partners commissioned eight Croatian artists to spend time in the area and then produce works based on their experiences. These pieces include Roberta Patalani's vast bas-relief, which anchors the promenade level lobby; Danijel Srdarev's ink illustrations; and the landscape photographs by Veronica Gaido that hang in the 209 rooms. Lissoni kept these private spaces simple, blending them into the hotel's natural surroundings through clay-hued wool rugs and warm woods on the raw concrete walls and floors. In every room and suite, glass doors open onto a balcony with the forest or sea beyond. —**C.R.**

Grand Park Hotel Rovinj

Helvetia & Bristol Firenze – Starhotels Collezione

Florence, Italy

A Florentine favorite since the late 1800s, the Helvetia & Bristol Firenze expanded in 2021 to include the adjacent former headquarters of Banco di Roma. The resulting 89-room property features the Helvetia wing's 64 classically opulent rooms and suites, as well as 25 contemporary rooms in the Bristol wing, the latter by the London-based actress turned interior designer Anouska Hempel. Public spaces have been meticulously restored as well, with old master paintings, original antiques, a winter garden (where breakfast is served), and floral chinoiserie wallpapers.

Though influenced by local palazzo architecture, Hempel's rooms feature a more pared-down aesthetic of pale oak herringbone floors, marble intarsia tables, sumptuous gray silks, and an array of mirrors. The expansion also includes the 5,813-square-foot (540-square-meter) La Spa, the largest in the city. Inspired by the ancient Roman baths that once stood here, the subterranean space incorporates both hot and cold treatments, a hammam, a Finnish sauna, a Vichy shower, salt rooms, and two pools. Travertine marble lines treatment rooms that once served as bank vaults, and a glass floor has been installed to allow a view of the medieval ruins below.

Set in the historic city center, steps from the fashion boutiques along Via Tornabuoni and the historic Piazza della Repubblica, the hotel draws guests and locals alike to its lavish Cibrèo Restaurant & Cocktail Bar, designed by the Roman architect Massimo Adario and featuring raised Ionic columns, a graphic checkerboard floor, red lacquered chandeliers, and an ethereal backlit marble bar. From dawn through *aperitivo*, the Helvetia & Bristol remains a true Tuscan treasure.
—**C.O.E.**

Hotel de Mar,
a Gran Meliá Hotel

Mallorca, Spain

Hovering over its own exclusive cove, Hotel de Mar, a Gran Meliá Hotel harks back to an era of grand entrances, generous rooms, and balconies large enough for loungers. Designed in 1964 by Josep Antoni Coderch, one of Spain's most noted postwar architects, this seven-story landmark received a thorough makeover in 2016 that updated areas indoors and out. With just enough midcentury touches, such as the white Verner Panton Cone Heart chairs in the "Red Level" lounge, it pays homage to its origins while ensuring that it meets contemporary needs.

The 137 rooms, 23 of which are suites, are light-filled and feature a palette of whites and golden browns that emphasize the surrounding natural beauty. "Red Level" rooms, meanwhile, offer access to a private lounge and afford complimentary use of the "Bali Beds" dotting the impeccable lawns. The flying-wing layout, tipping toward the sea, creates private, stepped balconies. Set in mature landscaping, the two pools are compact, but with the Mediterranean and a small beach at the end of the gardens, they are better suited to lazing than laps.

Of the four in-house restaurants—including all-day dining at Amaro, Mediterranean bites at Perseo, and Bardot's seafood by the sea—Arrels especially enchants. Here, the tasting menu devised by chef Marga Coll, who also runs Miceli in nearby Selva, adds a contemporary twist to Mallorcan classics, and changes daily depending on whatever she finds fresh in the market that morning. —**W.S.B.**

Hotel de Mar, a Gran Meliá Hotel

Hotel Metropole Monte-Carlo

Monte-Carlo, Monaco

A Belle-Époque treasure built in 1886, the majestic Hotel Metropole Monte-Carlo sits close to the central Place du Casino and the glamorous shops and restaurants of the Carré d'Or. After a thoughtful renovation by the French architect Jacques Garcia in 2004, the property now features a velvet-swathed lounge as part of its historic lobby bar. Famous for its manicured gardens—thought to have inspired Edith Wharton's *House of Mirth*—the hotel continues to epitomize elegance.

The 125 rooms feature mahogany-and-marble finishes and floral silks. The pièce de résistance is the 2,099-square-foot (195-square-meter) Suite Carré d'Or, a maximalist, terraced penthouse with sweeping views of the principality and the Mediterranean beyond. The Didier Gomez–designed Spa Metropole by Givenchy—one of just three Givenchy spas in the world—provides a true urban oasis with a botanical LCD display, 10 sleek treatment rooms, a hammam, a sauna, and a caldarium.

Gourmets are spoiled for choices among the hotel's four restaurants, including Les Ambassadeurs by Christophe Cussac, whose creative tasting menus pair harmoniously with Jacques Garcia's luminous dining room in shades of cream and gold, with rich ebony and stone finishes. The poolside Odyssey restaurant, featuring the late Karl Lagerfeld's theatrical, monochromatic vision, offers up a sublime study in graphic black and white. Equally opulent is the seawater-pool deck area, where Lagerfeld covered one wall with 18 fresco-style glass panels depicting the journey of Ulysses. **—C.O.E.**

Il Sereno Lago di Como

Torno, Italy

The Milan-based Spanish architect and designer Patricia Urquiola, known for her playful, suave style, envisioned the design of Il Sereno Lago di Como on the shores of Lake Como. The younger sibling to the beachfront Le Sereno Hotel, Villas & Spa on the Caribbean island of St. Barthélemy (page 58), this sleek sanctuary stands out among the grand, glamorous hotels that dot the shoreline, with its striking stone, walnut, and glass façade that sensitively situates itself within its surroundings.

Taking inspiration from the nearby Casa del Fascio, by the rationalist architect Giuseppe Terragni, Il Sereno's 40 minimalist rooms celebrate the changing natural light reflecting off the water throughout the day. Further enhancing these spaces are Urquiola's choices of finishes, including geometric Ceppo tiles, custom silks, a Canaletto walnut staircase lined with copper, and dark green Verdi Alpi stone. In the sprawling Signature Penthouse Suite are archetypal Italian furniture pieces by Cappellini, Franco Albini, Gio Ponti, and others.

Exteriors blend vertical gardens by the noted French botanist Patrick Blanc and a heated freshwater infinity pool by the lake. The small yet comprehensive spa is housed in an old *darsena*—Italian for "boathouse"—where guests relax in the unadorned sauna and steam rooms. Another special treat: the hotel's custom Cantiere Ernesto Riva boats, as well as the Vaporina del Lago, with its Urquiola-designed interiors in rich shades of blue and green. Overlooking the glistening lake is the vegetable-forward restaurant Il Sereno Al Lago, which features Venetian terrazzo-and-travertine stone floors as well as soaring Moltrasio stone arches that add to the *dolce vita* vibe.
—**C.O.E.**

J.K. Place Roma

Rome, Italy

An eight-year search led hoteliers Ori Kafri and Eduardo Safdie to the 17th-century townhouse, part of the Palazzo Borghese, that would become J.K. Place Roma, which opened in 2013 along a cobble-stone lane off Via dei Condotti. Known for his residential-style hotel interiors, here the Florentine interior designer Michele Bönan synthesized the *dolce vita* of the Eternal City in the 1950s and '60s with a contemporary élan. In the living room–like lobby, which looks up to a 21-foot (6.4-meter)-tall conservatory-style glass roof, Bönan honors Rome's rich history with classical statuary and a 17th-century Salvator Rosa framed fireplace, juxtaposed with his own low-slung sofas lined with beige Dedar fabric and delicate ground lamps made for Estro. Modern artworks including a 1970s Nerone and Patuzzi sculptural wood panel grace the walls.

In the clubby adjacent lounge, a backlit onyx wall and retro marble countertop bar face an alcove lined with polished rosewood panels where large-scale photos of 1970s beach houses by Gwathmey Siegel & Associates Architects hang above cream banquettes and ebony round tables with brass finishings. Beyond sits the decadent JKCafe, with its lemon-yellow walls in one dining room and emerald green in the next. Royal-blue velvet couches throughout are lined with white trim and crimson-hued, low-backed leather chairs lie beneath white recessed ceilings hung with 1960s Sputnik lamps.

Even the elevator becomes a salon, its L-shaped elephant-gray velvet sofa an unexpected, thoughtful gesture, especially on a hot summer's day. Polished rosewood reappears in all 27 individually designed rooms and suites, some with soaring bed canopies and all with Massimo Listri's majestic architectural photographs. —**C.R.**

Kulm Hotel St. Moritz

St. Moritz, Switzerland

Nestled in the Engadin Valley, overlooking Lake St. Moritz, the Kulm Hotel St. Moritz has been welcoming fashionable guests and outdoor enthusiasts alike since 1856. A Belle Époque gem, the property has seen enhancements over the years, including the addition of a 21,528-square-foot (2,000-square-meter) spa and an exquisite restoration of the original ice pavilion by Foster + Partners with the addition of a skating rink, a sculptural cantilevered canopy, and a restaurant and sun terrace—all incorporating locally sourced larch, ash, and stone.

A modern alpine aesthetic pervades the 150 rooms and sumptuous suites reimagined by interior architect Pierre-Yves Rochon using a palette reflective of the surrounding scenery, with pops of deep indigo and scarlet. Artisans from the Graubünden region worked in stone pine, as well as Vals granite, to create these serene interior spaces. Restaurants Sunny Bar by Tom Booton and Kulm Country Club, the latter bedecked with vintage bobsleds and assorted sports memorabilia, offer guests everything from regional mountain dishes to international cuisine.

A destination for both summer and winter pursuits, St. Moritz has a long sporting history, having hosted Switzerland's first and second Winter Olympics in 1928 and 1948, respectively. The legendary Cresta Run, a toboggan track added to the Kulm property in the winter of 1884–85, continues to draw intrepid athletes, while challenging pistes and the Snow Polo World Cup are perennial favorites. For a combination of pristine peaks, diverse cultural programming, and design-led architecture that seamlessly blends indoors and out, the Kulm Hotel St. Moritz embodies Swiss precision and St. Moritz pleasure. —C.O.E.

Kulm Hotel St. Moritz

L'oscar London

London, United Kingdom

The decadent and ornate L'oscar London takes its name from the witty 19th-century poet and playwright Oscar Wilde, who in his time was both a literary sensation and a known appreciator of the finer things, once famously remarking, "Oh, would that I could live up to my blue china!" The hotel's moniker also nods to the site's historic literary locale: Nestled inside the former London headquarters of the Baptist Church, the hotel sits along Southampton Row in an area long associated with the "Bloomsbury Group" of thinkers including Virginia Woolf, John Maynard Keynes, and E.M. Forster.

Fittingly, the first thing guests see upon entering these theatrical environs, which feature lavishly appointed Baroque interiors by the French architect Jacques Garcia, is the lobby to the right, designed as an elegantly outfitted library; opposite is the gilded, mirror-covered L'oscar Restaurant, and, toward the back of the hotel, the Baptist Bar. The most resplendent space, however, may be the 818-square-foot (76-square-meter), wood-lined Committee Room upstairs, featuring a Royal Doulton terra-cotta plaque carved in 1903 and depicting a scene from John Bunyan's *The Pilgrim's Progress.*

The first hotel in London from the French hospitality entrepreneur Michel Reybier, L'oscar London features 39 rooms, 18 of which are suites. The hotel's most playful and Wilde-esque element is, without question, the flock of 495 yellow-crystal parakeets, kingfishers, and hummingbirds affixed throughout, perched on a ceiling light here, a sconce there, and practically fluttering about. Rich in color, texture, and materiality, this hotel also seduces with its custom scent from the British perfumer Roja Dove: a sweet, leathery musk that Wilde no doubt would have reveled in. **—S.B.**

L'oscar London

La Réserve Paris – Hotel and Spa

Paris, France

Text by **Cynthia Rosenfeld**
Photography by **Gaelle Le Boulicaut**

F og may be synonymous with London, but Paris records a surfeit of gray days from late fall to early spring, too. Thus, to come upon the fire engine–red door of La Réserve Paris – Hotel and Spa, as I did one sleepy Sunday afternoon in late November, was to experience the tingly sensation of becoming Alice, just as she steps through the looking glass. And so it was that I left behind the City of Light's ashen autumnal landscape and entered a kaleidoscopic wonderland from which none of Paris's innumerable attractions could lure me out.

For the hotel's interior designer, Jacques Garcia—also responsible for La Réserve's sister properties in Geneva and Ramatuelle (for Ramatuelle, see page 207), and L'oscar London (previous spread), among many other sumptuous spaces—red symbolizes blood, and therefore life. The color appears in many guises throughout the 40-room property, the smallest of Paris's 12 "palace" hotels, a distinction bestowed by the French government based on aesthetics, historical value, service standards, and gastronomy.

Fairy tale–style, I entered an astonishing world inspired by masterpieces of art and architecture. Each guest is welcomed at the hotel's Louis XV Salon, modeled by Garcia on the Grand Salon of Napoleon III apartments at the Louvre, from its gilded ceiling cornices embellished with angels to its central round banquette upholstered in a scarlet floral damask. A faded oxblood Oriental rug warms the square room, leaving exposed at its edges the geometric-patterned Versailles parquet oak floor imported from a Loire Valley chateau and named for the flooring in Versailles's Hall of Mirrors.

Amidst this formal grandeur, owner Michel Reybier had Garcia add framed Reybier family photos atop an ornate console inherited from Reybier's grandmother. More of these intimate tableaus adorn the walls on the upper five floors, adding a personal touch that reinforces Reybier's philosophy—manifest across all four La Réserve hotels, including at its Philippe Starck–designed Zurich location—of making guests feel as if they have been invited to stay in one of his homes.

In 2012, the French entrepreneur bought this *hôtel particulier*—as grand, single-family Parisian townhouses used to be called—in the city's Eighth Arrondissement, on the Avenue Gabriel, named after Ange-Jacques Gabriel, who created the public square that is now Place de la Concorde for King Louis XV. It's a surprisingly discreet setting, given its location just steps from the heavily fortified French presidential palace, the touristy Champs-Élysées,

and the couture houses along Rue du Faubourg Saint-Honoré and the Avenue Montaigne. Built in 1854, in the Second Empire style of Baron Georges-Eugène Haussmann—the architect celebrated for reimagining modern Paris—for Napoleon III's half-brother, Charles-Auguste-Louis-Joseph, Duc de Morny, the six-story building hosted friends that the duke invited to parties at the then exclusive establishments along the Champs-Élysées. Reybier purchased the mansion from the estate of the fashion designer Pierre Cardin, then hired Garcia and the architect Bach Nguyen, who oversaw the structural restoration and modern additions including an underground floor. The extensive, three-year renovation employed more than 120 artisans, some borrowed from the Louvre's ateliers, and required 250 tons of marble and nearly 20,000 feet (6,000 meters) of fabric. The resulting La Réserve Paris debuted in 2015.

Inhaling the hotel's signature fragrance—a subtle mélange of cedar, mahogany, and patchouli—I followed a hotel butler along the maroon-carpeted white marble staircase that curves around a central chandelier inspired by those in the private apartments at Versailles. All 15 rooms and 25 suites are lavishly outfitted in silk damask walls, velvet drapery, gilt-framed mirrors, and the Point de Hongrie herringbone parquet floors that, for me, emblematize Paris. A quartet of floor-to-ceiling windows in the suite I stayed in made for unobstructed views of the Eiffel Tower and the Grand Palais, the massive Beaux-Arts complex built for the 1900 Paris Exposition. Naturally, I took a seat at one of the private balcony's two French café tables and spent that evening watching the Eiffel Tower

La Réserve Paris – Hotel and Spa

**Opposite, top
to bottom**
The bedroom of the
Eiffel Presidential
Suite.

The hotel's Duc de
Morny Library features
3,000 books available
for guests to borrow.

sparkle, as it does for five minutes every hour until midnight. Inside, surrounded by a low-slung, chocolate-brown velvet loveseat and armchairs, the ebony-lacquered coffee table was laden with goodies: an edible chocolate Eiffel dusted bronze with sugar powder; a pyramid of clementines; a champagne bucket full of Alain Milliat exotic juices; haut marshmallows the color of fresh snow; and four chocolate-covered, pecan-infused madeleines.

After the Eiffel's lights were extinguished, I slipped into the oversize bathtub and admired the vast bathroom, clad entirely in Turquin blue and Carrara white marble, the latter slashed with black and gray veins that recall a Jackson Pollock painting. Garcia's favorite shade makes an appearance even here, in the jewelry box varnished a deep vermilion. This is not to mention the suite's other thoughtful touches: underfloor heating in the bathroom, a maxi-size minibar stocked with wine from the owner's Bordeaux vineyards, and Devialet speakers, which I used to wirelessly stream lullaby-like playlists as I snuggled between the smooth Quagliotti linens.

The next morning, I took the long way downstairs to admire some of the hotel's 200-plus works on paper by early-20th-century caricaturist Georges Goursat—better known as Sem—whose amusing drawings-as-social-commentaries featuring Belle Époque bourgeoisie such as John Pierpont Morgan and Baron James Mayer de Rothchild line the wine-colored hallway walls. Back on the ground floor for breakfast in La Pagode de Cos restaurant, as copious plates of fresh fruit and French breads were served, I was distracted by the flamingo-hued onyx columns that Garcia had imported from Rajasthan and the dining chairs' upholstery: a tropical, pistachio-shaded tapestry festooned with flowers and peacocks that he adapted from the 1866 oil painting *Cercle de la rue Royale*, by the artist James Tissot, which hangs across the Seine in the Musée d'Orsay. Throughout the day and evening, La Pagode de Cos serves seasonal French cuisine laced with Asian flavors, including a grilled octopus with Thai spices that instantly transports one to a Bangkok street market.

Next door is the Duc de Morny Library, a high-ceilinged refuge of elegant marquetry and green velvet couches. Along with paintings and sculptures from Reybier's personal collection, three thousand French titles—both contemporary and historic, meant to be borrowed by guests in residence—fill these shelves. At the far end sits the Cos Room, a snug, three-sided vestibule displaying ornate antique Indian birdcages alongside glass jars of Asian spices and historic photos of Reybier's Château Cos d'Estournel wine estate, designed by Louis Gaspard d'Estournel with three Chinese-style rooftop pagodas.

After sipping on a glass of COS100, made from a parcel of 100-year-old merlot vines planted at Cos d'Estournel by women during the first World War, and bottled in 2015 to celebrate the winery's 100th anniversary, I spied the discreet door leading to the Winter Garden. The lounge, reserved for members and hotel guests only, centers around a selection of 400 cigars housed in a custom gray-leather Pinel et Pinel humidor, styled like a vintage steamer trunk, set upright and open to display cherry-red shelves stocked with Cohibas, Romeo y Julietas, and Montecristos. Hand-painted by the trompe l'oeil artisans from Atelier Mériguet-Carrère, the longtime Yves

Saint Laurent collaborators, the walls and ceiling evoke an old-fashioned, glass-walled conservatory looking out upon an idyllic French countryside.

Back near the hotel's entrance sits the two-Michelin-starred fine dining restaurant Le Gabriel, an elegant, formal space made comfortable and contemporary with embossed leather walls and an abstracted leopard-spot carpet designed by Garcia. Elsewhere in the hotel, guests will continue to discover even more secrets, semi-hidden like Easter eggs, including the hushed, subterranean spa specializing in Nescens-Swiss anti-aging treatments, where I descended for a midnight swim in the 52-foot (16-meter)-long heated pool—a rarity in Paris. Walls lacquered candy-apple red lead to a hammam, a trainer-staffed fitness studio, and three treatment rooms.

My final hours were especially sweet, with the hotel's general manager inviting me to a *chocolat chaud* tasting in Le Gaspard bar, festive with locals on a weekday at 5 p.m. We bypassed its impressive wine list—some 500 white and more than 1,000 red labels—to test the hot chocolate concocted by the hotel's Brittany-born executive chef, Jérôme Banctel, who has added crisped buckwheat, a staple of his native region, to my favorite Parisian treat. The small, private club–like bar offers an abundance of design delights, from the gilded ceiling details; to the Doric columns behind the leather-clad bar; to the 19th-century mirrors blackened with mercury; to one of the building's five original fireplaces, its blush marble veined gray and white and carved with a central scalloped seashell; to a deftly rendered battle scene cut into the blackened interior wall.

Gold-painted elephants stood guard overhead as we carried out our mission.

Sipping the molten, caramel-infused Patrick Roger chocolate liquid, I marveled at the highly choreographed teamwork dedicated over the past several months to crafting this single guest experience—from the chef who trained at the celebrated L'Ambroisie in Place des Vosges and under Alain Senderens at Lucas Carton, to the pâtissier creating the accompanying powder sugar-dusted beignets, to those involved in choosing the porcelain service and designing the presentation. To each guest who stays at this exquisitely run hospitality operation, one thing quickly becomes abundantly clear: La Réserve Paris is a dream come true.

Opposite
The Louis XV Salon, modeled on the Grand Salon of Napoleon III apartments at the Louvre museum.

This page
The dining tables at Le Gabriel spread at generous intervals atop a Jacques Garcia-designed carpet.

La Réserve Ramatuelle – Hotel, Spa & Villas

Ramatuelle, France

An early 2000s restoration of a 1970s building with a bold, modernist pagoda roofline akin to the Fondation Maeght art museum in Saint-Paul-de-Vence, La Réserve Ramatuelle – Hotel, Spa & Villas nestles in the hills near the coastal town of Saint-Tropez. From inside the ochre-hued, curved-edged structure, the Mediterranean Sea, fringed by *chêne-liège* and pine trees, captivates through floor-to-ceiling windows. Michel Reybier, the French entrepreneur behind La Réserve, instructed the Paris-based architect Jean-Michel Wilmotte to prioritize nature when rehabilitating this abandoned structure for the hotel's 2009 opening. Wilmotte obliged by opening up all eight rooms and 19 suites to full sea views and even integrating the hillside's craggy limestone along the main structure's hallway and 10,764-square-foot (1,000-square-meter), sea-facing spa.

For renovations that began in 2021, Reybier encouraged the French designer Jacques Garcia to lean in to the Côte d'Azur's sublime light. Garcia placed white leather Hans Wegner Papa Bear chairs around the color-free lobby where white ceramic sculptures provide depth without adding distraction. He celebrated the French Riviera's Belle Époque style in the individual hand-painted mural for each guest room and borrowed from the region's color palette for the bed textiles. Fourteen three-to-seven-bedroom Provençal peach-hued villas feature arched doorways and terra-cotta floor tiles.

Jean Lurçat's naïf ceramic plates from the 1950s and '60s depicting roosters and moons clad the far wall inside Restaurant La Voile's otherwise pared-down dining room. A 10-minute drive leads to La Réserve à la Plage, designed by Philippe Starck for barefoot brunching, with natural fiber hanging lamps and rustic wood tables wedged into the sand. **—C.R.**

LeCrans

Crans-Montana, Switzerland

Set high above the pine-forested ski village of Crans-Montana, the 14-room LeCrans effortlessly fuses Swiss tradition with contemporary design. Originally opened in the 1960s, the four-level property has been transformed by the Swiss architect Grégoire Comina, with local larch, Valais and Lucerna stones, and slate, to create a grand yet intimate-feeling chalet that remains faithful to the regional vernacular.

The interiors reflect these staggeringly beautiful surroundings, with floor-to-ceiling windows and a soothing, neutral palette highlighting unobstructed views of Mont Blanc, the Weisshorn, and the Matter Valley beyond. Belgian designer Christophe Decarpentrie looked to the world's highest peaks and mountain ranges—Annapurna, Oural, and the Dolomites among them—for inspiration in the guest rooms and suites, each one individually designed using art and furnishings from around the globe. The Rocky Mountains Prestige Suite is just one example of the attention to detail here, with Canadian maple, imported textiles, and a wood-burning fireplace all lending a North American feel. Various soft touches, such as bearskins, marmot fur, and chamois, are found throughout, as are antlers, ornate mirrors, and antique furniture.

Public spaces, including the Michelin-starred LeMontBlanc, feature brushed-oak floors and expansive, circular windows, creating a light-filled atmosphere ideal for savoring chef Yannick Crepaux's inventive tasting menus. Vietnamese green stone and slate clad the indoor lap pool in the spa, which also hosts a heated outdoor pool poised over the treetops. While the design pays homage to the world's sky-piercing peaks, in every part of the hotel—from cozy, chalet-inspired niches to dining and bar areas to the fitness suite— its own endless Alpine panoramas are the real stars of the show.
—C.O.E.

LeCrans

Le K2 Chogori

Val-d'Isère, France

Composed of just two chalets containing nine flexible suites and two penthouses, Le K2 Chogori may be small, but it packs a mighty punch. Admittedly, its location in the magnificent Val d'Isère gives it a head start, but the hotel does all the heavy lifting. This personal project—the owners, the Capezzone family, are local—feels more private home than hotel, thanks to scion Thomas, who subverts expected aesthetics with a palette of Alpine slate grays and muted woods, offset by touches of Tibet, soft golds, oranges, and pops of Nyingma red. The curios, art, fabrics, and generous furnishings introduced by his mother, Suzanne, create a cocoon-like feel in the rooms, which are view-oriented and visually various, emphasizing the private-home vibe.

In a far cry from the usual mountain fare of raclette and *tartiflette*, the in-house restaurant L'Altiplano specializes in spicy, flavor-forward Peruvian dishes based on locally sourced ingredients, and Le 1954 Bar—named for the year K2 was first summited—serves meals in addition to drinks. Other facilities include a sleek gray marble lap pool, a hammam, a jacuzzi, and a sauna to soothe muscles after a strenuous day on the slopes, while the Goji Spa, named after the fruity "red diamonds" of the Himalayas, has a focus on anti-aging treatments.

With its multiple nods to other high-altitude regions, Le K2 does not hide its appreciation for the high life. From the slopes at Tignes, to summer skiing on the Pisaillas glacier, to Isère's network of hiking trails, this lavish, intimate retreat is tailor-made for lapping up its beautiful surroundings. —W.S.B.

Lido Palace

Riva del Garda, Italy

Riva del Garda, a cobblestoned town on the northwestern tip of Lake Garda, Italy's largest freshwater lake, has lured artists, thinkers, and royalty alike for over a century with its turquoise waters and stately mountains. Many, if not most, have found their respite there within the walls of Lido Palace. A stone's throw from the shore and surrounded by plunging cliffs, the hotel grants privacy and serenity well-paired with its Mediterranean hospitality.

The regal, 19th-century villa rests on a manicured plot lined with verdant cypresses and palms escorting guests to its entrance. Its Neoclassical façade includes mirrored wings containing 42 modernized rooms in a style hinted at by the conservatory-like lobby. Constructed at the peak of Europe's Belle Époque, Lido Palace has continued to bend toward the avant-garde under architect Alberto Cecchetto's 2011 renovation, which elegantly married glass walls with stone exteriors on the ground and top floors.

Toward the back of the property, a sweeping sheet of Cor-Ten steel and the garden's dense branches shelter the hotel's lake-view dining area, as well as its dual heated pools, which are fenced in by curvilinear chaises longues. The upper level's aptly named Sky Suites features immersive panoramas framed by slate-gray tones and minimalist lines. Deep soaking tubs sit window-side in some of these upper-level suites, maintaining impressive views throughout. Winds delivered from the Dolomites, meanwhile, provide optimal conditions for sailing out beyond the palatial grounds and exploring the region's quaint villages and rolling vineyards. —**H.M.**

Lido Palace

Lily of the Valley

La Croix-Valmer, France

It was a meeting of minds when the French business executive Alain Weill tapped the architect and designer Philippe Starck to master-plan his 53-key hotel, Lily of the Valley, southwest of Saint-Tropez. Together, they conceived a startlingly different spot from many of the grande dame hotels nearby, instead creating a luxe riff on a classic Provençal village sitting in its own, artfully overgrown grounds, the tendrils of greenery that wreathe the buildings lending them a centuries-old patina. One room stands apart, quite literally: Villa W, a three-bedroom *maison* that dates back to the 1950s and that Starck restored to its mid-century heyday, complete with a private pool tiled in jazzy black, red, and yellow on the terrace, and an Eames Executive chair inside—a subtle nod to the fact that Starck hopes that the entire place evokes the home Charles and Ray designed for themselves in Pacific Palisades in the late 1940s.

The resort's raison d'être is the *art de vivre*, that French take on wellness that manages to celebrate instead of punish. The 21,528-square-foot (2,000-square-meter) spa at the heart of the hotel is its anchor, and offers everything from hammams and snow showers to deep-tissue massages and LED therapy. (The actress Catherine Deneuve's former private therapist oversees the regimens here.) It was Weill's own attempts to find a place where he could upgrade his fitness after turning 50 that inspired the entire undertaking. Since no spa satisfied him, he resolved to create his own, in collaboration with his onetime fashion exec daughter. Guests can opt to follow what Lily of the Valley dubs its "Shape Club" wellness and weight-loss program—one of their four health offerings—eating food so delicious they hardly notice their treatments. The hotel, being French, naturally encourages a daily glass of red wine. —M.E.

Mezzatorre Hotel & Thermal Spa

Forio d'Ischia, Italy

One of the Phlegraean trio of islands in the Gulf of Naples, Ischia is home to the Aragonese watch-tower, half-built during the 16th and 17th centuries, which later became the Mezzatorre Hotel & Thermal Spa (*mezzatorre* translates as "half-tower"). The classic carnelian-hued gem with its neo-Moorish crenellation rising above the pine forest–covered headland at the island's northwestern tip received a head-to-toe makeover in 2019 by the celebrated hotel impresario Marie-Louise Sciò, the CEO and creative director of her family's Pellicano Group, which also owns Hotel Il Pellicano along the Tuscan coast and La Posta Vecchia outside of Rome.

Sciò revamped the main Ristorante La Torre with Pierre Frey L'esterel wallpaper that echoes the land-scape, along with an intricately patterned wood parquet floor. The seascape reigns underneath a giant palm frond palapa at the simpler beach grill, where direc-tor's chairs are covered with blue, black, and white fabric, and nothing but a rustic wood fence comes between diners and the blue-green Tyrrhenian Sea, with Mount Vesuvius in the distance. Ischia's own volcano feeds the thermal hot springs flowing into three effervescent pools in the spa, with its herringbone, bottle-green wall tiles and whitewashed mud rooms. Sunseekers congregate around the green quartzite–floored swim-ming pool and also below, under pink umbrellas along two curving stone terraces that hug the rocky promontory above the hotel's secluded bay.

Housed mainly in the tower that once watched for marauding Saracen pirates, with a scattering of low-rise, rosy-hued bungalows across the hillside, all 48 rooms and suites boast tantalizing sea views. Under vaulted ceilings, white-canopied beds pop with colorful custom ikat and *suzani* print runners or bold-patterned Manuel Canovas headboards. —**C.R.**

Mezzatorre Hotel & Thermal Spa

Mezzatorre Hotel & Thermal Spa

Myconian Imperial Resort

Mykonos, Greece

Inside the hard stone–clad and dazzling white exterior of the family-run Myconian Imperial Resort, plaster rhinos, silver owls, and other unusual tchotchkes in the lobby express the hotel's relaxed vibe. As do the sprinkling of clever-kitsch "I (Heart) Mykonos" cushions and moss-covered chandeliers in the gardens. The work of set-designing duo Antonis Kalogridis and Vangelis Takos, this is whimsy for grown-ups.

The 111 rooms lean rustic-chic, and that's because this is the island of Mykonos, where there aren't many reasons to be indoors, other than to rest, wash up, or slip into something spectacular. The interiors are also largely white, which lends the floor-to-ceiling views of the Aegean (and the sunset) a cinematic quality. The luminous surfaces are interrupted by wood details that vary from room to room, and include floating tables and desks; slender log ceilings and behind-the-bed walls; black panels; the occasional splash of colorful upholstery; and soft, rounded white furniture straight out of Stanley Kubrick's *2001: A Space Odyssey*.

The closest hotel to Elia Beach, where it claims its own private section, and within striking distance of shuttles to the main town and the party beaches elsewhere on the island, the resort also runs shuttle services to its sister properties, giving guests access to an even wider range of restaurants and wellness facilities, not that—with its swim-up bar and jewel-like spa—the Imperial gives them much reason to leave. —**W.S.B.**

Palacio Arriluce Hotel

Getxo, Spain

Along the Vizcaya Coast in Spanish Basque country, with views of the Nervión Estuary flowing into the Cantabrian Sea, a former palace designed in the neo-Gothic style by the Bilbao architects José Luis de Oriol y Urigüen and Manuel María Smith for the Marquis of Arriluce in 1912 became the Palacio Arriluce Hotel in 2023. Built of ashlar stone, this stately building is bracketed by a duo of asymmetrical towers linked by a recessed central structure. On the colonnaded ground floor, bay windows jut out dramatically. Restored over four years by Madrid's International Hospitality Projects (Grupo Plan), the imposing palace evokes the region's history and also sits less than 20 minutes by car from the Frank Gehry–designed Guggenheim Museum Bilbao and Santiago Calatrava's Bilbao International Airport.

AHB Estudio and Grupo Plan transformed the interiors, channeling the hotel's aristocratic tenants in each of the 49 individually designed rooms, some housed in the former pergola. Salvaged marquetry, moldings, and stained-glass windows are complemented by antique tapestries belonging to the Marquis's family, with plump modern armchairs and sofas that encourage lingering. The hotel's art collection includes pop art by Victor Vasarely, Eduardo Chillida engravings, and a commissioned Diego Canogar sculpture titled *Arriluce Embraces*. A cocktail lounge inhabits the erstwhile library and chapel, its altar transformed into the present-day bar, while the restaurant Delaunay honors the hotel's Sonia Delaunay engravings and prints.

Outside, atop the cliffs of the Bay of Abra, sloping gardens surround the hotel, which is encircled by retaining walls with blind arcades. Bracketing the property are the sunset-facing pool terrace and an internationally accredited croquet lawn that hosts championship matches. **—C.R.**

Palacio Arriluce Hotel

Palacio Arriluce Hotel

Portrait Milano

Milan, Italy

Text by **Maria Cristina Didero**

Initially constructed in the 16th century, this former archiepiscopal seminary has been home to the resplendent Portrait Milano hotel since 2022. While Milan has long been renowned for its dynamism (as with the Teatro alla Scala opera house), creativity (a design and fashion capital, it's home to the headquarters of brands such as Prada, Giorgio Armani, and Ermenegildo Zegna), and unwavering spirit (embodied by the Duomo, which dates back to the 14th century), Portrait Milano has swiftly expanded its reputation as a hub for highly refined, world-class hospitality. Discreetly nestled in the bustling city's heart—just a minute's walk to Piazza San Babila—the hotel stands as a quiet-luxury treasure, an exquisite establishment that leans into its historic setting steeped in local heritage.

As a result of a meticulous, decade-long overhaul by the illustrious Ferragamo family, founders of the famed Florentine

Previous spread
Portrait Milano's
10_11 bar and library,
designed by Michele
Bönan.

Opposite
The patio of 10_11,
which looks out to
the garden.

fashion empire and the owners of the six-hotel Lungarno Collection, this hotel has undergone a remarkable structural transformation inside and out. Upon entering the elegant, glamorous space, guests will feel as if they have been suddenly whisked onto a modern-day Fellini film set.

The story of Portrait Milano traces back to 1564, when Carlo Borromeo, the archbishop of Milan from 1564 to 1584 and a cardinal of the Catholic Church, commissioned the building as one of the world's earliest seminaries. It has served various purposes throughout its history, from a library to an educational institution, and even housed the architect Mario Bellini's office from 1980 to 1990. In the 17th century, the addition of a grand courtyard and a majestic Baroque portal by Francesco Maria Richini elevated this already impressive structure to the monumental status of an architectural masterpiece. As decades and centuries passed, however, the seminary gradually receded from the limelight, fading into relative obscurity—until it was reawakened for its metamorphosis into this bastion of best-in-class hospitality.

From conception, the hotel's vision revolved around promoting inclusivity and reimagining the historical site as an accessible treasure for all to enjoy. Notably, the renamed Piazza del Quadrilatero, with its impressive Baroque gates standing wide open, serves as a welcoming pedestrian pathway connecting two distinct urban realms: the exclusive Corso Venezia and the high-end shopping street of Via Sant'Andrea. As a result, Piazza del Quadrilatero, spanning 30,139 square feet (2,800 square meters), stands as the largest square within this fashionable neighborhood. Adorned with a grand entrance and an elegant colonnade, it hosts two retail boutiques, two restaurants, and a bar.

To bring this stately vision to life, two renowned Micheles—the Milan-based architect and designer Michele De Lucchi and the Florence-based interior designer Michele Bönan—came together, each lending his distinct and complementary talent to the project. Internationally celebrated for his pared-down perspective and humanistic touch, as well as his elegant use of natural materials, De Lucchi was the perfect choice to oversee the transformation of this space from a private, closed-off sanctuary to an inviting and open environment for all—guests and locals alike—to enjoy. Meanwhile, Bönan, a longtime collaborator with the Ferragamo family, crafted a warm and intimate interior ambience, striking a harmonious balance with the grandeur of the building.

The second floor of the palazzo, inscribed with intricate engravings of the motto "Humilitas" (or humility, the Borromeos' family maxim) on its walls, fosters a regal atmosphere, and, as with the other upper floors, is accessible only to hotel guests. With 73 rooms and suites ranging from a cozy 344 square feet (32 square meters) to a magnificent 1,776 square feet (165 square meters), the hotel offers a range of accommodations to satisfy various needs. Options range from the Portrait Studio and Studio Deluxe for two guests to the opulent Borromeo Suite, a two-bedroom suite for up to six. Upon walking in, these resplendent spaces awe visitors with their elaborate details and distinguished décor. The rooms and suites frame the astonishing grand loggia and boast courtyard

Opposite, top to bottom
The guest rooms recall Milan's 1950s parlors with their use of walnut wood and rattan paneling.

The Longevity Spa draws inspiration from the building's 16th-century origins and features 10 granite columns that rise from a cistern-like pool.

and garden views. (The garden, with its array of beautifully crafted wicker lounge seating, serves as an ideal breakfast location.)

Beyond its extraordinary design, the hotel is also an impressive engineering feat, with each of the stained-glass windows it holds in place weighing a staggering 1,760 pounds (800 kilograms). The interiors draw inspiration from the 1950s parlors of Milan and feature Italian walnut. The superlative Florentine craftsmanship shines through in details such as leather and bronzed brass handles, natural larch flooring, and marble-clad bathrooms. Throughout, the dominant color scheme revolves around shades of dark red and green—standby Tuscan references—and through an array of photographs and graphic artworks, the property pays homage to Milan's rich legacy from the past half century.

The Longevity Spa provides yet another opportunity for Portrait Milano to pamper its guests within its breathtaking setting. The wellness area, located underground in a part of the building that dates to the Middle Ages, features a pool shaped around a series of the original columns. It is the perfect place to enjoy Italian *viaggi*, or journeys, designed for both physical and mental health.

The decision to establish Portrait Milano in the center of Milan carries profound significance within the broader narrative of the Lungarno Collection, three of which are fellow Portraits—this one along with Florence and Rome—all of them members of The Leading Hotels of the World. For each of these projects, the mission is to devise a distinctive "portrait" of the place it inhabits. It's not merely about creating another luxury hotel; it's about sculpting an immersive experience that resonates with the very soul of its surroundings.

As such, throughout the property, special details that honor the city's history abound. Take the aperitifs, for example, such as the ready-to-go Ambrogino, the Milano-Torino, or the Milano Martini, which nod to 1960s Milanese mixology. Or consider the gastronomic offerings that highlight traditional Italian dishes—a must is the three-ingredient *pasta in bianco*, at once straightforward yet complex in flavor. Upon entering the ground floor, a rich array of delights await at 10_11 restaurant and bar (so called because it fetches two street addresses, on both Corso Venezia and Via Sant'Andrea); the first Beefbar to open in Italy; and Rumore, a destination for mixology and live music, complemented by two fashion boutiques: Antonia, an upscale fashion and accessories store, whose floor is a beautiful concrete parquet designed by the Italian architect Vincenzo De Cotiis, as well as the first flagship store of So-Le Studio, designed by Fondamenta Studio, which features Maria Sole Ferragamo's sophisticated jewelry creations.

With this diverse ensemble of offerings, the hotel serves as a lively showcase for the very essence of the cosmopolitan destination it calls home. Portrait Milano is not merely a hotel, but a living embodiment of Milan's vibrant past and present. An animated cultural epicenter, it is a striking symbol of inclusive and multifaceted hospitality.

This page
The Executive Suite, which incorporates a deep shade of cardinal red as a tribute to St. Charles Borromeo, the cardinal who established the former seminary.

Opposite
Inside the 10_11 restaurant and bar.

Opposite
The garden at
the 10_11 restaurant
and bar.

This page
The hotel's Piazza del
Quadrilatero interior
courtyard.

Principe Forte dei Marmi

Forte dei Marmi, Italy

If *la dolce vita* were a place, it would be Forte dei Marmi. The seaside town first rose to prominence in the postwar period, when wealthy Milanese families such as the Fiat-owning Agnellis co-opted it as their weekend getaway, creating a fantasy of glamour that even Visconti might have struggled to dream up. Today, Forte dei Marmi remains that city's answer to the Hamptons in New York, luring the likes of Miuccia Prada and Giorgio Armani to buy homes here.

Principe Forte dei Marmi sits on its own grounds, set back slightly from the road, a few blocks south of the center of town. The 28-room hotel was designed by the German architect Klaus Müller, who fashioned far larger rooms than the ones found in the typical classic hotel in this area: Each is at least 323 square feet (30 square meters) in size, with clean modern furniture, including geometric four-poster beds from an assortment of high-end Italian brands such as B&B Italia.

Though the hotel has two pools, in this part of Italy, daytime life centers on the lido. Forte dei Marmi's highly manicured and well-maintained beach clubs are surrounded by huge swaths of gorgeous golden sand leading down to the Mediterranean. Dalmazia is the exclusive-use club for Principe's guests, a mere three-minute walk away. Guests can book one of the 40 or so gazebos for the day, and need budge only for a quick dip or to grab lunch under an umbrella at the club's buzzy restaurant. —**M.E.**

Ritz Paris

Paris, France

In 1898, the Swiss hotelier César Ritz opened the Ritz Paris on the Jules Hardouin-Mansart–designed Place Vendôme, with then-innovative en suite bathrooms, telephones, and centralized power switches. For the 2016 reopening, the French-born, New York–based architect and designer Thierry Despont mobilized classic French craftsmanship, with the hotel also working with the likes of Pierre Frey for custom fabrics, carpets, and rugs; Christofle for silverware; Baccarat for crystal glassware; and Haviland for porcelain tableware.

The gilded lobby offers an intoxicating display of chandeliers, tufted chairs, antiques such as a Regency amaranth marquetry chest in red serpentine marble with stylized dragon pulls, and a majestic staircase with a polished brass and gilt-iron balustrade. Despont removed the original mezzanine level to create 18-foot (5.5-meter) ceilings, which allow light to stream in through a high oval window. The Espadon Restaurant opens onto a Burgundy limestone terrace facing the Grand Jardin, where Despont and the landscape architect Jean Mus lined the 17,222-square-foot (1,600-square-meter) Versailles-style park with lime trees, hornbeam hedges, pruned boxwoods, and white magnolias and jasmines, adding small alcoves for intimate cocktail rendezvous.

Teatime includes madeleines in the aptly named Salon Proust, with its red velvet chairs beneath carved French oak walls. The 25-seat Bar Hemingway pays homage to the eponymous American writer. He and other Ritz habitués, including 34-year resident Coco Chanel, are immortalized in 16 Prestige Suites among the 142 generous accommodations. Color schemes of ivory and pale pinks or blues are accented by rich brocades and Louis XV furnishings. In the marble bathrooms, the golden swan taps are a small but enduring signature.
—C.R.

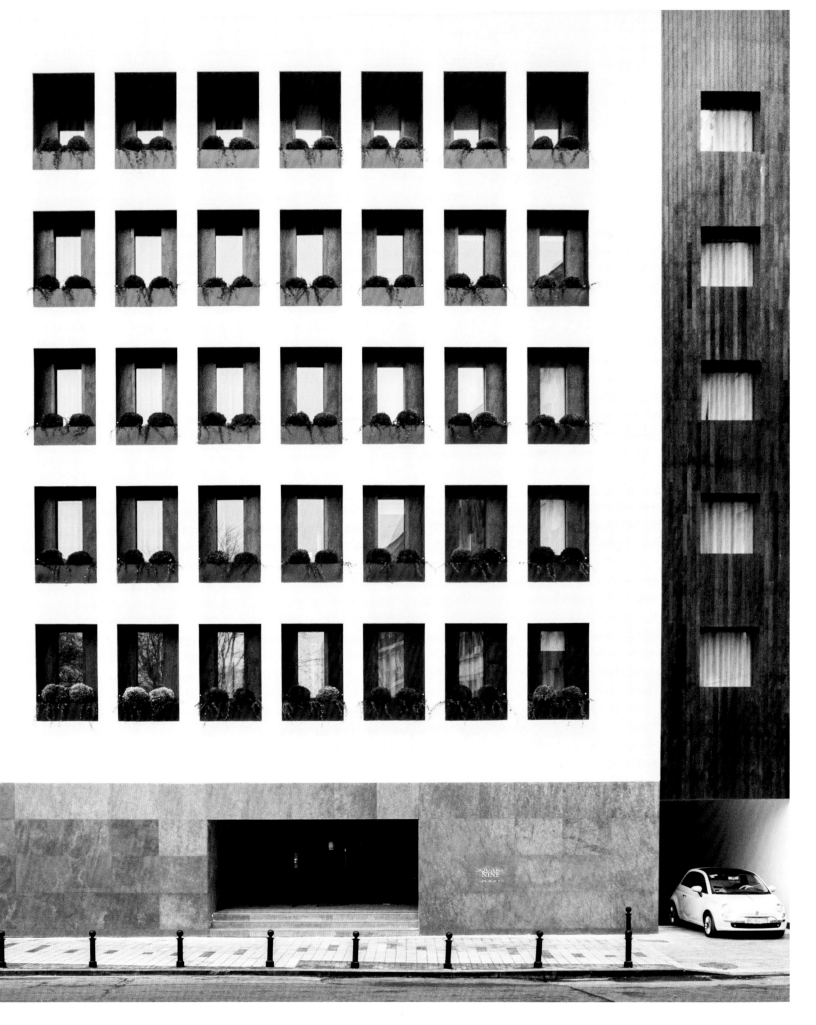

Square Nine Hotel Belgrade

Belgrade, Serbia

To create Square Nine Hotel Belgrade, in the heart of Belgrade's Stari Grad historic quarter, Serbian brothers and owners Nenad and Nebojsa Kostic reached out to the São Paulo–based architect Isay Weinfeld. The property, which opened in 2011, would become Weinfeld's first hotel outside of South America. For the project, Weinfeld eschewed any glaringly contemporary construction to follow the scale and rhythm of the surrounding Secessionist-style buildings. His orderly, Bauhaus façade of stone and imported Brazilian rosewood neatly blends with the area's muted exterior hues.

The ground-level, midcentury-vibe lobby centers on a bar lined with original Arne Vodder rotating, green-leather stools. The décor is a veritable time capsule, with original Hans Wegner chairs, Poul Kjærholm PK31 armchairs, Edward Wormley's Dunbar furnishings, a Bruno Mathsson four-seat sofa, and Oscar Niemeyer's Mesa table, interspersed with brass lamps and vintage globes on a patchwork of time-worn Persian carpets. Repairs were upholstered with Loro Piana fabrics or Edward Green leather. The Square restaurant, too, reso-nates with nostalgia, with its sepia photographs of old Belgrade and leather chairs around tables dressed in white linen.

Upstairs, wood-, stone-, and leather-clad hallways are furnished individually with Scandinavian and North American pieces dating to the 1930s through the '60s. The 30 rooms and 15 suites blend Cumaru wood wall panels, Portuguese Crema Europa lime-stone, and oak wood floors, and are softened by linen wallpaper, Turkish rugs, underfloor heating, and cash-mere throws. —**C.R.**

Tschuggen Grand Hotel, Arosa

Arosa, Switzerland

Surrounded by 140 miles (225 kilometers) of ski runs in southeast Switzerland at an altitude of 5,906 feet (1,800 meters), the Tschuggen Grand Hotel, which dates back to 1929 and includes a 2006 spa extension designed by the Swiss architect Mario Botta, operates the Tschuggen Express, a slickly engineered funicular of circular cabins that whisks guests to the skiing and hiking of Arosa Lenzerheide in under four minutes. Inside the unassuming eight-story room block, Swiss architect and designer Carlo Rampazzi brings his trademark maximalist touch, lacquering the ceilings in an alpine-summer jade green and the copper and burnt orange of fall-colored leaves. Above the bed covers, embroidered with stylized snowflakes, checkerboards of contrasting textiles climb the walls in many of the 128 individually decorated rooms.

For the spa, called Bergoase, Botta—who trained under Le Corbusier and Louis Kahn, and who is perhaps best known for his design of the San Francisco Museum of Modern Art, as well as for his 2004 and 2023 renovations of the La Scala opera house in Milan—slipped most of the luminous structure beneath the surface, leaving the wilderness untouched. Nine geometrically organic sails of titanium, zinc, and glass rise out of the ground, their walls channeling daylight into the four-story, 53,820-square-foot (5,000-square-meter) spa complex. At night, these modernist Moai are illuminated to dramatic effect. Below the soaring volumes lie a dozen treatment rooms, fitness studios, whirlpools, and a hivelike sauna. On the top floor, an exterior sauna, solarium, and swimming pool further connect guests with Arosa's awe-inspiring environs. —**C.R.**

Tschuggen Grand Hotel, Arosa

Tschuggen Grand Hotel, Arosa

Villa Maïa

Lyon, France

Although it sits within a UNESCO World Heritage site first settled in 43 B.C.E. and around the corner from a Roman amphitheater, Villa Maïa's 2017 opening coincided with the completion of artful contemporary edifices by David Chipperfield, Herzog & Meuron, and Kengo Kuma in Lyon's nearby Confluence neighborhood, an urban renewal project at the meeting point of the Rhône and Saône rivers.

Close to the pinnacle of Fourvière Hill, with its unhindered views of the French Alps, Villa Maïa was designed by the French architect Jean-Michel Wilmotte, who conceived this four-story historical homage in opaque glass and concrete. Inside, another Frenchman, the interior designer Jacques Grange, best known for the homes of Yves Saint Laurent and Karl Lagerfeld, crafted the 34 rooms and suites in a soothing spectrum of oatmeal to mushroom, masterfully blending Japanese straw-lined walls and mouth-blown glass from La Verrière de Saint-Just with custom, Art Deco-inspired furniture in marble and wood. Anamorphic artwork by Charles Maze hangs above each bed. Louis Benech planted the hotel's serene garden with wildflowers including iris, carnation, aniseed, and bitter almond, all of which are infused in the custom, Grasse-made amenities for the bathrooms. Generous windows offer 180-degree panoramas of Lyon's red rooftops, with Mont Blanc in the distance.

Wilmotte hews closest to the area's antiquarian heritage with the 66-foot (20-meter) heated indoor swimming pool lined with Doric columns and arched windows, its marble deck derived from an ancient mosaic unearthed on this site during archeological excavations. —**C.R.**

Villa Nai 3.3

Žman, Croatia

On the island of Dugi Otok, a sliver of land off the Dalmatian coast roughly equidistant from Dubrovnik and Venice, the Croatian architect Nikola Bašić and Villa Nai 3.3's owner, the civil engineer Goran Morović, carved eight accommodations directly into a hillside overlooking the Adriatic Sea. The excavated stones were repurposed for interior and exterior walls constructed according to the UNESCO-protected Dalmatian tradition of dry stacking without mortar, which also reduces carbon dioxide emissions.

The hotel's 10-acre (four-hectare) site sits within a 500-year-old olive grove, itself surrounded by the Aleppo pine and oak forests of three national parks, and its name reflects this rich history: *nai* means "snow" in the old Dalmatian language, and 3.3 was the average number of days of annual snowfall here centuries ago, ideal for a bountiful olive harvest. The hotel operates a mill that produces Morović's award-winning organic olive oil, and every October, guests are invited to participate in the harvest.

Bašić designed the villa in a cave to resemble a moored yacht, symbolizing his belief that sailing establishes a heightened intimacy with nature. The furniture, all fabricated by the Italian design company Giorgetti, is intentionally understated, to keep the focus on the natural surroundings, just as the sunroof in each bathroom is designed for this remote outpost's exceptional stargazing. Rooms all open onto private terraces, with views of the olive grove or the Adriatic. The two on-site restaurants include the 18-seat Grota 11,000, an open-air gastro-ode to wood-fire grilling—of meat, fish, and vegetables sourced on the island and offshore—as was the custom 11,000 years ago. —**C.R.**

Vinha Boutique Hotel

Vila Nova de Gaia, Portugal

Fifteen minutes from Porto's historic center, on nine exquisitely gardened acres (3.6 hectares) along Portugal's Douro River, sits the fashion-forward Vinha Boutique Hotel, developed by siblings Rui and Joana Poças. A trained architect, Joana completely transformed the 16th-century terra-cotta-colored manor house, adding a low-rise contemporary structure derived from the gentle slopes along the Douro. Interiors throughout feature European antiques, vintage furniture, and items from Joana's travels.

Downstairs in the speakeasy-style Reserva Bar, where the all-glass wall behind the bar offers captivating river views, shades of the area's wine sumptuously varnish the walls and appear in velvet on the high stools. Eyes travel upward at Vinha Restaurant, helmed by chef Henrique Sá Pessoa (who oversees all of the hotel's gastronomic offerings), where Moooi's riotous "Extinct Animals" wallcovering adorns the recessed ceiling above gargantuan Chinese cloisonné vases, burnished mirrors, rattan-embellished chairs, and a floor of green marble imported from Brazil. At Sá Pessoa's more casual Terroir Brasserie, coral-washed walls contrast with electric-blue accordion screens, painted ceramic heads, and cane dining chairs in a glossy Chinese red lacquer.

Each of the 38 individually designed rooms evokes Joana's playful nature, as well as her love of fashion. Take the cozy twin-bed rooms: One is finished with Ralph Lauren-esque tartans, the other covered in Manuel Canovas's toile de Jouy prints. River-view rooms highlight Italian fashion house Etro's haute-hippy spectrum or Maison Pierre Frey's clashing prints while suites nod respectively to Missoni, Kenzo, Christian Lacroix, and architect and illustrator Nigel Peake's 2013 "Promenade au Faubourg" design for Hermès.
—C.R.

Widder Hotel

Zurich, Switzerland

Nine medieval townhouses thoughtfully combined by the Swiss architect Tilla Theus comprise the Widder Hotel in Zurich's Old Town. Opened in 1995 after a decade-long renovation, the property features 49 light-filled rooms and suites, each a fusion of past architectural styles. Theus restored the original structures' Roman, Gothic, and Biedermeier features, along with the enormous rough-hewn oak beams, grisaille frescoes, and stucco work, all enhanced by contemporary architectural and high-tech touches, including state-of-the-art glass elevators and floor sensors that activate night lights. Although the disparate buildings connect via discreet passageways, each retains its distinct identity through Theus's use of a specific type of wood and stone for each structure.

Public and private spaces here feature museum-quality furniture by Le Corbusier, Mies van der Rohe, Eileen Gray, Charles and Ray Eames, and Frank Lloyd Wright. The art collection, with works by the likes of Hans Arp, Alberto Giacometti, and Andy Warhol, graces the walls of the hotel's library, the Widder Restaurant, and the *boucherie*-brasserie-bistro August. A site-specific work by Robert Rauschenberg adorns the duplex penthouse suite, which also features a terrace with 360-degree views of Zurich's church spires and cobblestone streets.

For fitness enthusiasts, the subterranean wood-paneled gym stays in keeping with the Widder's overall minimalist aesthetic. The 10th-century Steinhaus—the oldest building in the complex—houses a private library stocked with books about Zurich and the arts, as well as comfortable Eames loungers that encourage reading and relaxation. Part medieval museum, part art and design gallery, the Widder Hotel stands mere steps away from the bustling Bahnofstrasse yet feels a world apart. —**C.O.E.**

Widder Hotel

Index

Explore the entire **Leading Hotels of the World** collection. Plus: Insider recommendations from influential voices in design and hospitality, and the editors' picks of what to do when in Berlin, Istanbul, and beyond.

WHEN IN MENDOZA...

The **O. Fournier** winery (Calle Los Indios s/n Valle de Uco), designed by the Mendoza-based architecture firm Bórmida & Yanzón, reflects its Spanish owner's desire to showcase the drama of his New World wines and facilitates his gravity-driven wine-making process. Under the colossal, aerodynamic steel roof supported on four hollow concrete columns, grapes get gently crushed into juice that descends into fermentation tanks, after which the wine trickles into the cavernous, below-ground wine cellar, which doubles as an art gallery.

—The Editors

PRO TIP: HONG KONG

"Stroll back in time around the **Kadoorie Estate** in Kowloon. Start from Mong Kok, one of the world's densest neighborhoods. Minutes later, you'll arrive at this unexpectedly serene enclave of mid-twentieth-century houses—many of them Bauhaus in style—set among beautiful old banana and banyan trees. Coming here perpetuates such a different sense of Hong Kong for me."

—André Fu, architect and founding principal, André Fu Studio

Fauchon L'Hôtel Paris
4 Boulevard Malesherbes, Paris, France ↓

Hôtel Barrière Fouquet's Paris
46 Avenue George V,
Paris, France

**Hôtel Barrière
Le Grand Hôtel Dinard**
46 Avenue George V,
Dinard, France

**Hôtel Barrière
Le Majestic Cannes**
10, La Croisette, Cannes, France

Hôtel Barrière Le Royal
Boulevard Cornuché, Deauville, France

Hôtel Barrière Les Neiges
422, Rue de Bellecôte, Courchevel, France

Hotel Byblos
20 Avenue Paul Signac, Saint-Tropez, France

Hotel Casadelmar
Route de Palombaggia, Porto-Vecchio, Corsica, France

Hôtel Chais Monnet & Spa
50 Avenue Paul Firino Martell, Cognac, France ↓

Hotel Château du Grand-Lucé
7 Place du Château, Le Grand-Lucé, France

Hotel Royal – Evian Resort
960 Avenue du Léman, Évian-les-Bains, France

Hotel Royal-Riviera
3 Avenue Jean Monnet, Saint-Jean-Cap-Ferrat, France

J.K. Place Paris
82 Rue de Lille, Paris, France

**La Réserve de Beaulieu,
Hôtel & Spa**
5 Boulevard du Maréchal Leclerc, BP 49, Beaulieu-sur-Mer, France

---

PRO TIP: SAINT-TROPEZ

"At the border between Ramatuelle and La Croix-Valmer, **Cap Taillat** is a sandy isthmus sheltered by a rocky promontory. Standing there makes you feel like you're moving between two vast seas. Reach it by land, on foot, or by bicycle (or electric mountain bike, from Lily of the Valley), or by sea in a kayak. If you are observant and patient, you might spot a Hermann's tortoise, the only terrestrial tortoise in France. As the aperitif hour approaches, make your way to **Le Sube** (15 Quai Suffren), an intimate spot at the Saint-Tropez harbor. Climb the stairs to find the cozy club chairs, the mahogany bar, and the small terrace overlooking the boats, with the most breathtaking view of the city at sunset, best enjoyed with a drink in hand."

—Lucie Weill, owner, Lily of the Valley

WHEN ON THE CÔTE D'AZUR...

Few, if any, homes offer as much intrigue and allure as the modernist villa **E-1027** (Sent. Massolin, Roquebrune-Cap-Martin), which has been meticulously restored by the Cap Moderne foundation that operates it and provides guided in-depth tours. Designed by Eileen Gray and completed in 1929, this shiplike structure—dramatically perched along the southern coast of France between Monaco and the Italian border—is without question one of the most remarkable examples of architecture from the 20th century.

—The Editors

WHEN IN BERLIN...

There's no art space in the world quite like the **Feuerle Collection** (Hallesches Ufer 70), two floors of exquisitely illuminated rooms designed by the masterful minimalist John Pawson inside a former World War II telecommunications bunker. Presenting a private collection of antiquities from Southeast Asia and China and international contemporary art, these extraordinary, by-appointment-only galleries leave a lasting impression.

—The Editors

Avant Mar (page 126)
Piperi Beach, Naoussa Paros, Cyclades, Greece ↓

PRO TIP: ATHENS

"A Neoclassical building hosting the world's most extensive collection of artifacts from the Cyclades islands, dating back to six thousand years ago, the **Cycladic Art Museum** (Neofitou Douka, 4) features representations of ancient Greek culture so refined and contemporary as to be influential on fashion trends today. At the **Public Tobacco Factory** (Lenorman 218), there's a not-to-be-missed contemporary art gallery inside an astonishing building. For lunch or dinner, go to **Avli** (Ag. Dimitriou 12), which serves traditional Greek food in a really unexpected scenario, along a tiny street of the Monastiraki neighborhood."

—Paola Navone, architect and designer

PRO TIP: SANTORINI

"A short stroll from the Katikies Kirini Santorini in Oia, the **Byzantine Castle Ruins** stand as a silent yet eloquent witness to the island's rich history. Echoing the cultural depth of the island, these ruins offer a breathtaking panorama of Santorini's past. Established in the medieval times, this historical site, also known as the castle of Agios Nikolaos, was once the heart of the island's aristocratic life. Today, what remains is a poignant reminder of the bygone Byzantine era. Its walls, though worn by time, still resonate with ancient stories. Visitors are particularly drawn to the ruins at sunset, when the sky and the Aegean Sea merge into a spectacle of colors, framing the place in an almost ethereal light. The ruins not only provide a stunning view, but also a serene spot for reflection."

—Vasileios Koumpis, general manager, Katikies Hotels

PRO TIP: BALI

"Pejaten Village's **Tanteri Ceramics** (Br. Simpangan, Desa Pejaten Kediri, Tebanan) is a living testament to Balinese craftsmanship. Visitors can witness skilled artisans breathe life into clay, molding it into exquisite pottery, tiles, and art pieces that celebrate tradition and innovation.

"Still inhabited by royal descendants and built in traditional Balinese architectural style, the seventeenth-century **Kerambitan Palace** (Jalan Pahlawan Lejeh, Desa Baturiti, Kerambitan, Tabanan) is the cultural seat of a village of the same name. It's located in Bali's fertile southwest, which has its own *tektekan* trance dance, believed by locals to have magical powers."

—Soo K. Chan, architect and owner, Soori Bali

PRO TIP: VENICE

"Not far from the Baglioni sits one of my favorite museums in Venice—a complicated statement because there are so many, and there's so much to see here. However, the **Museo di Palazzo Grimani** (Castello Ramo Grimani 4858) is a jewel and certainly not on everyone's list. It's imperative to see the display room of Roman antiquities—the Tribuna Grimani—collected by Giovanni Grimani in the sixteenth century. It's extraordinary, and has been wonderfully restored by the nonprofit Venetian Heritage."

—Rodman Primack, art adviser, co-owner of AGO Projects,
and principal of the of the design firm RP Miller

WHEN IN PUGLIA...

Housed in a 17th-century bishop's residence, **Epiphany Society** (Via degli Ammirati 6, Lecce) is a linen lair where the best buys range from easy-to-pack bread baskets and slouchy, oversized totes to natural-dyed bedding and table covers.

—The Editors

PRO TIP: MILAN

"Founded in 1971, the antiquarian jewelry boutique **Gioielleria Pennisi** (Via Alessandro Manzoni 29) comes from a family of jewelers and diamond collectors who decided to focus on antique pieces. Here you can discover one-of-a-kind and extremely rare finds, from the 1700s to the modern day, with particular emphasis on Art Deco. I've purchased many magnificent pieces for my wife at Gioielleria Pennisi, including her engagement ring: an antique Indian ring with a central emerald and enamel details."

—Romeo Gigli, fashion designer

PRO TIP: NAPLES

"Naples feels like a jewel box of historical eateries and backdrops meant for visitors to enjoy from any seat for hours. One of my favorite places is **Gran Caffè Gambrinus** (Via Chiaia 1). A landmark from the nineteenth century, the café, hidden at the rear of the Palazzo della Prefettura, features to breathtaking murals, people-watching, and delicious pastries and coffee. Then, in one of the oldest districts in the city, down a long cobblestone alley, is **Da Concettina ai Tre Santi** (Via Arena alla Sanità 7 Bis), a fourth-generation, family-operated pizzeria devoted to superior-quality ingredients and to the Neapolitan people. With more than sixty years of experience feeding artists, their local community, and countless visitors, the magic behind the Oliva family is how they continue to strive toward modernization and reimagining their vision of the world through their cooking.

"Within a stone's throw of the Grand Hotel Vesuvio, you'll find a row of modern furniture stores that for a second make you think you're in Milan. One in particular, **Galerie Caiafa Arte** (Via Chiatamone 6/G), has a curation that makes it hard to resist wanting to ship the entire lot. The owner, Massimo Caiafa, has a family connection to the arts dating back to the 1600s. The shop stocks Gio Ponti, Sergio Asti, and Gino Sarfatti, to name a few, and carries a variety of works, from lighting and chairs to sculptures and beyond."

—Beverly Nguyen, boutique owner and fashion stylist

PRO TIP: FLORENCE

"Since its founding, in 1896, the restaurant/ concept shop/florist **La Ménagère** (Via de' Ginori 8/R) has been a Florentine favorite. Once a housewares emporium, the convivial boutique has been reimagined by the design firm Q-Bic into ten rooms, including a bright breakfast café that morphs into a sceney bar by night. Vintage furnishings, Karman lighting, and contemporary objects are juxtaposed with original vaulted ceilings to create a wholly original, design-led destination."

—Christina Ohly Evans, U.S. correspondent, *HTSI*

Le Sirenuse
Via Colombo 30, Positano, Italy ↓

Palazzo Roma
Via del Corso 337, Rome, Italy

Palazzo Venart Luxury Hotel
Santa Croce 1961, Venice, Italy

PRO TIP: VENICE

"An old-school printing atelier, **Gianni Basso Stampatore** (Calle del Fumo 5306, Cannaregio) specializes in exquisite, custom-designed cards, bookplates, and stationery. Gianni, who is known as 'the Gutenberg of Venice,' also operates a museum of letterpress-printing instruments next door."

—Brooke Hodge, curator and writer

The PLACE Firenze
Piazza Santa Maria Novella 7, Florence, Italy

Portrait Firenze
Lungarno Acciaiuoli 4, Florence, Italy

Portrait Milano (pages 231–39)
Corso Venezia 11, Milan, Italy

Portrait Roma
Via Bocca di Leone 23, Rome, Italy

PRO TIP: RAVELLO

"The **Museo del Corallo** (Piazza Duomo 9), only a few minutes' walk from Palazzo Avino, is one of my favorite places in Ravello. The 'Camo,' founded by Giorgio Filocamo and now in the hands of his daughter Tiffany, is a treasure trove of historic coral pieces handmade and engraved by Filocamo himself, blended with beautiful cameos and other jewelry. Its setting itself, underneath the **Duomo di Ravello**, is an experience and a step back into the past."

—Mariella Avino, managing director, Palazzo Avino

PRO TIP: MILAN

"The **Chiostri dell'Umanitaria** (Via Francesco Daverio 7) stands as a precious historic gem in the heart of Milan, a resilient testament to memory that miraculously endured the bombings of World War II. Dating back to the fifteenth century, this former Franciscan convent, adorned with four adjoining cloisters, is a significant example of Renaissance architecture. The entire venue, with its expansive internal gardens and rich history, has become dear to my heart."

—Paola Lenti, furniture designer

Principe Forte dei Marmi
(page 241)
Viale Amm. Morin 67, Lucca, Forte dei Marmi, Italy

Relais San Maurizio
Località San Maurizio 39, Santo Stefano Belbo, Italy

Relais Santa Croce by Baglioni Hotels
Via Ghibellina 87, Florence, Italy

WHEN IN FORTE DEI MARMI...

The quarries of Carrara are the ultimate place to begin any Italian vacation, and when in Forte dei Marmi, a **Carrara Marble Mine Tour** (Via Fantiscritti 2, Carrara) is a must. Call ahead to book a private trip up the mountain in a Land Rover; you'll be whisked up several switchbacks and suddenly find yourself surrounded by massive walls of white marble and, if you're lucky, with your head literally above the clouds. After the tour, drive five minutes down the road to the ancient village of Colonnata, and stop by **Bar Merenderia Larderia da Mario** (Via Fossacava 27) to taste some of the town's famously sweet, pearl-colored lardo. Aged in marble vats inside the mountain grottoes, the incredibly creamy salume melts instantly in your mouth. Pair it with bread, slices of tomato, and a cold beer for the full effect.

—The Editors

Royal Hotel Sanremo
Corso Imperatrice 80, Sanremo, Italy

San Clemente Palace Kempinski Venice
Isola di San Clemente 1, Venice, Italy

Santavenere
Via Conte Stefano Rivetti 1, Maratea, Italy

Terme di Saturnia Natural Spa & Golf Resort
Località Follonata, Tuscany, Saturnia, Italy

Therasia Resort Sea & Spa
Località Vulcanello, Isola di Vulcano, Lipari, Italy

Verdura Resort, a Rocco Forte Hotel
S.S. 115, Km. 131, Sciacca, Agrigento, Italy

Villa Agrippina, a Gran Meliá Hotel
Via del Gianicolo 3, Rome, Italy

Villa Cora
Viale Machiavelli 18, Florence, Italy

PRO TIP: FLORENCE
"The **Rucellai Chapel** (Via della Spada 40) is a hidden gem of Florence. In my beloved city, which is full of masterpieces of art and so many heavily trafficked museums, the opportunity exists to discover this treasure thanks to the Place of Wonders foundation. If you book a visit to the **Museo Marino Marini** (Piazza San Pancrazio), you can make a donation to a scholarship fund for young artisans in Florence, and after a visit to the museum, a door to the usually closed Rucellai Chapel will open. (The museum occupies the deconsecrated part of the church of San Pancrazio.) There, you'll see a Holy Sepulcher masterpiece by Leon Battista Alberti, created for Giovanni Rucellai's tomb.

"Just around the corner from the Place Firenze, there's **Hunter Vintage** (Via del Moro 56), a very special vintage store for fashionistas and collectors where the owner, Tommaso Pampaloni, is a Florentine reference for many fashion designers. He has access to one of the largest vintage archives in Europe."

—Claudio Meli, general manager, The Place Firenze

Villa d'Este
Via Regina 40, Lake Como, Cernobbio, Italy →

Villa del Parco & Spa
S.S.195, Km. 39.600, Santa Margherita di Pula, Cagliari, Sardinia, Italy

Villa Eden – The Private Retreat
Via Winkel 70, Merano, Italy

Villa e Palazzo Aminta
Via Sempione Nord 123, Lake Maggiore, Stresa, Italy

Villa La Massa
Via della Massa 24, Candeli (Florence), Italy

Violino d'Oro
San Marco 2091, Venice, Italy

Jamaica

Mammee Bay Resort Jamaica
Lot 2, Mammee Bay, Jamaica

Japan

Espacio The Hakone Geihinkan Rin-Poh-Ki-Ryu
72 Miyanoshita, Hakone-machi, Ashigarashimo-ku, Kanagawa, Japan

Fauchon Hotel Kyoto
406 Namba-cho, Shimogyo-ku, Kyoto, Japan

Halekulani Okinawa (page 92)
1967-1 Nakama, Onna-son, Kunigami-ku, Okinawa, Japan

The Hotel Seiryu Kyoto Kiyomizu
2-204-2 Kiyomizu, Higashiyama-ku, Kyoto, Japan

PRO TIP: TOKYO
"A gallery with two different spatial expressions on opposite sides of a street in the old town Asakusabashi district, **Hakujitsu** (1 Chome-24-1 Yanagibashi, Taito-ku) practically slips through time, bringing one's attention to the beauty of craft across generations."

—Stephanie Goto, architect

PRO TIP: KYOTO
"Whenever I'm in Kyoto, I repeat my pilgrimage to the potter and poet **Kawai Kanjirō's House & Studio** (569 Kaneicho, Gojozaka, Higashiyama-ku). The traditional architecture and furniture, and the simple layout of the buildings, are always inspiring. The seven-chamber Noborigama kiln gives you a sense of the magnitude and commitment of what it meant to be a studio potter at that time. Anyone enchanted by the process of pottery should pick up a copy of his book of poems. His language around his process never ceases to reignite a sense of magic around the material.

"I also recommend knife shopping in Aya Zaimokucho: My two favorite knife shops are on the same Sakaimachi-Dori Street, near the markets in Kyoto. For excellent customer service and more variety of blades and handle types, head to **Yagi Houchouten** (540 Yaoya-cho, Nagagyo-ku). My personal favorite is a few blocks south, at **Hayakawa Hamonoten** (Higashimaecho, Shimogyo Ward), a tiny, funkier shop where the process is on full view. It's run by an older knifemaker who is good-spirited and extremely patient. Also check out **Kawataki Kyoto Kitchen Shop** (505 Masuyacho, Nakagyo-ku) for beautiful ceramics and kitchenwares, and **Ichihara Heibei Shoten** (118-1 Koishi-cho, Shimogyo-ku) for chopsticks and utensils."

—Simone Bodmer-Turner, ceramicist and sculptor

Imperial Hotel, Tokyo (page 95)
1-1 Tokyo Uchisaiwai-cho, 1-chome, Chiyoda-ku, Tokyo, Japan

The Kahala Hotel & Resort Yokohama
1-1-3, Minatomirai, Nishi-ku, Yokohama, Japan

The Okura Tokyo (pages 103-11)
2-10-4 Toranomon, Minato-ku, Tokyo, Japan

Palace Hotel Tokyo
1-1-1 Marunouchi, Chiyoda-ku, Tokyo, Japan

"Designed by the artist Hiroshi Sugimoto, **Sasha Kanetanaka** (Oak Omotesando 2F, Kita-Aoyama 3-6-1, Minato-ku) makes me want to move to Tokyo. The eloquence and beauty of this restaurant—itself as much a work of art as the Sugimoto pieces hanging on its walls— awes, and the incredible food is served in portions so small you don't feel gluttonous ordering everything. The Japanese garden there completes the ambience, which is minimalist but feels absolutely resolved."

—Gulla Jonsdottir, architect

WHEN IN TOKYO...

We could easily come up with dozens of unforgettable things to do in Tokyo, but here we'll leave you with just two: the **Nezu Museum** (6 Chome-5-1 Minami-Aoyama, Minato-ku), which features a vast collection of ancient Asian art inside a heritage structure updated according to the principle of *wa*, or harmony, by the architect Kengo Kuma, and **Sogetsu Plaza** (7 Chome-2-21 Akasaka, Minato-ku), which offers reservation-only visits to the Japanese-American artist Isamu Noguchi's *Heaven* installation on the ground floor. Made of stones and water, the latter space is designed for presenting *ikebana* flower arrangements. Heavenly indeed.

—The Editors

"A meditative space for tea, **Haku** (570–210 Gionmachi Minamigawa, Hiashiyama-ku) opens portals of exploration into the seasonal beauty of Japanese ingredients, where one bite of their creations opens your eyes, expands your mind, and inspires you to contemplate deeper possibilities."

—Stephanie Goto, architect

Korea

Signiel Seoul (page 116)
Lotte World Tower 76F–101F, 300, Olympic-ro, Songpa-gu, Seoul, South Korea

WHEN IN SOUTH KOREA...

Near the Demilitarized Zone separating North and South Korea, hundreds of South Korean writers, artists, cineastes, architects, and musicians live and work in **Heyri Art Valley** (70–21, Heyrimaeul-gil, Paju-si, Gyeonggi-do). More than thirty museums operate here alongside various other cultural spaces.

—The Editors

The Shilla Seoul
249, Dongho-ro, Jung-gu, Seoul, South Korea ↓

"Situated in the beautiful residential area of Komaba, a few stations away from the bustling Shibuya neighborhood, is the **Japan Folk Crafts Museum** (4-3-33 Komaba, Meguro-ku). Founded by Yanagi Sōetsu, the leader of the Mingei Movement, this example of traditional Japanese architecture presents a combination of Japanese home and treasure chest. Ceramics, textiles, and wood crafts here are delights to the eye, and the museum shop offers curated craft gifts from different regions of Japan."

—Kulapat Yantrasast, architect

Latvia

Grand Palace Hotel
Pils. Street 12, Riga, Latvia

Luxembourg

**Le Royal Hotels & Resorts
– Luxembourg**
12 Boulevard Royal, Luxembourg,
Luxembourg

Malaysia

The Datai Langkawi
Jalan Teluk Datai, Langkawi,
Malaysia

Republic of Maldives

Baglioni Resort Maldives
Maagau Island, Dhaalu Atoll,
Republic of Maldives

Constance Halaveli Maldives
Alifu Alifu Atoll, Halaveli, Republic of
Maldives

Emerald Faarufushi Resort & Spa
Faarufushi Island, Raa Atoll,
Republic of Maldives

Emerald Maldives Resort & Spa
Fasmendhoo Island, Raa Atoll,
Republic of Maldives

Sirru Fen Fushi
Shaviyani Atoll, Republic of
Maldives

Malta

The Phoenicia
The Mall, Floriana, Malta

Mauritius

Constance Prince Maurice
Choisy Road, Poste de Flacq,
Mauritius

Maradiva Villas Resort & Spa
Wolmar, Flic-en-Flac, Black River,
Mauritius

Royal Palm Beachcomber Luxury
Royal Road, Grand Baie, Mauritius

Mexico

Alexander
Pedregal 24, Col. Molino del Rey,
Alcaldía Miguel Hidalgo, Mexico
City, Mexico

Casa Chablé
Carretera Federal Tulum, Km. 34.5,
Col. Javier Rojo Gomez, Punta
Allen, Quintana Roo, Mexico

Casa Polanco (pages 35–43)
Luis G. Urbina 84, Col. Polanco,
Polanco III, Miguel Hidalgo, Mexico
City, Mexico

PRO TIP: MEXICO CITY
"Just around the corner from
Casa Polanco is my favorite
chocolate shop in Mexico City,
Tour Chocolat (Avenida Emilio
Castelar 22). To get there, take
a lovely walk along Parque
Lincoln, a verdant green oasis
in the heart of the neighborhood. Founded by the famed
local pastry chef Luis Robledo
Richards, Tour Chocolat has
excellent chocolates, pastries,
and coffees. I'm addicted to the
dark chocolate–coated passion
fruit marshmallows!"

—Rodman Primack, art adviser,
co-owner of AGO Projects, and
principal of the of the design
firm RP Miller

Chablé Maroma
Carretera Federal 307, Km. 51,
Manzana 2, Lote 601, Ejido Norte,
Playa del Carmen, Quintana Roo,
Mexico

Chablé Yucatan
Tablaje 642, Chocholá, Yucatan,
Mexico

**Marquis Los Cabos All-Inclusive
Resort & Spa**
Carretera Transpeninsular Km. 21.5
Fraccionamiento Cabo Real, San
Jose del Cabo, Mexico

Marquis Reforma Hotel & Spa
Paseo de la Reforma No. 465,
Colonia Cuauhtemoc, Mexico City,
Mexico

Paradisus Los Cabos
Carretera Transpeninsular Km. 19.5,
San José del Cabo, Mexico

**Sensira Resort & Spa – Riviera
Maya**
Calle Tanchacte Lote 4-01, Puerto
Morelos, Quintana Roo, Mexico

UNICO 20°87° Hotel Riviera Maya (page 86)
Manzana 22 Carretera Federal 307, Km. 260, Solidaridad, Mexico ↓

Monaco

Hôtel de Paris Monte-Carlo
Place du Casino, Monte-Carlo,
Monaco

Hôtel Hermitage Monte-Carlo
Square Beaumarchais, Monte-Carlo,
Monaco

Hotel Metropole Monte-Carlo
(page 183)
4, Avenue de la Madone, Monte-
Carlo, Monaco ↓

Mongolia

Ayan Zalaat Hotel and Spa
Dunjingarav 1 Street, Entrance
No. 422, 11th Khoroo, Bayanzurkh
District, Ulaanbaatar, Mongolia

Montenegro

**Ananti Resort, Residences &
Beach Club**
Drobnici BB, Rezevici, Montenegro

The Chedi Luštica Bay
Marina Village Luštica Bay, Radovici,
Montenegro

Morocco

La Mamounia (page 17)
Avenue Bab Jdid, Marrakech,
Morocco ↓

Royal Mansour Casablanca
27 Avenue des Forces Armées
Royales, Casablanca, Morocco

Royal Mansour Marrakech
Rue Abou Abbas El Sebti,
Marrakech, Morocco

Royal Mansour Tamuda Bay
Route de Sebta, M'Diq, Tétouan,
Morocco

The Netherlands

De L'Europe Amsterdam
Nieuwe Doelenstraat 2–14,
Amsterdam, The Netherlands ↓

WHEN IN MARRAKECH...

Behind an unmarked gate in the Gueliz district, the Ibiza-based architects Diego Alonso and Alexeja Pozzoni stylishly reimagined a crumbling 1930s colonial vestige as the **Petanque Social Club** (74 Boulevard el Mansour Eddahbi), incorporating a hidden nook festooned with delightfully frenzied graffiti by the Moroccan painter Yassine Balbzioui. (Hungry? Try the feta-spinach pizza.) After taking over a contemporary art gallery in the same neighborhood for her namesake **Studio Sana Benzaitar** (8 Rue des Vieux Marrakchis), Benzaitar hired the architect Idries Karnachi to display her artfully nontraditional carpets—woven by Amazigh women in two Middle Atlas villages—as saddles hung over poles jutting from the whitewashed walls, an idea borrowed from Moroccan leather purveyors.

—The Editors

Hotel Des Indes
← Lang Voorhout 54–56, The Hague, The Netherlands

Hotel Okura Amsterdam
Ferdinand Bolstraat 333, Amsterdam, The Netherlands

Norway

The Dylan Amsterdam (page 163)
Keizersgracht 384, Amsterdam, The Netherlands

Britannia Hotel
Dronningens Gate 5, Trondheim, Norway

Hotel Continental
Stortingsgaten 24–26, Oslo, Norway

Oman

The Chedi Muscat (page 14)
North Ghubra 232, Way No. 3215, 18th November Street, Muscat, Sultanate of Oman

Pakistan

Islamabad Serena Hotel
Khayaban-e-Suhrawardy Sector G-5, Islamabad, Pakistan

Panama

Nayara Bocas del Toro (page 61)
Frangipani Island, Bocas Del Toro, Panama ↓

Peru

Country Club Lima Hotel
Los Eucaliptos 590, Lima, Peru

Portugal

Bairro Alto Hotel (page 129)
Praca Luis de Camoes No. 2, Lisbon, Portugal

Grande Real Villa Italia
Rua Frei Nicolau de Oliveira, 100, Cascais, Portugal

Hotel Quinta do Lago
Quinta do Lago, Almancil (Algarve), Portugal

Hotel Quinta do Paral
Quinta do Paral, Apartado 31, Selmes, Portugal

Maison Albar – Le Monumental Palace
Avenida dos Aliados 151, Porto, Portugal

Olissippo Lapa Palace
Rua do Pau de Bandeira, 4, Lisbon, Portugal

WHEN IN LIMA...

At her sunlit, by-appointment-only studio overlooking the Pacific Ocean, **Esther Ventura** (1157 Malecón Almirante Grau) pays homage to Peru through one-of-a-kind jewelry that incorporates *mullu*, the spondylus shell believed by native Peruvians to facilitate fertility, shiny red and black *huayruro* seeds coveted across the Andes as good luck charms, and pre-Columbian stone-carved animals from Nazca, evocative of the enigmatic geoglyphs etched into the earth there like ancient graffiti.

—The Editors

PRO TIP: SINGAPORE

"Singapore is not known for its secrets, but **D. Bespoke** (2 Bukit Pasoh Road) has always been a hideout for me. It's so private and comfortable. The lost-in-time charm reminds me of an old tailor in Tokyo's Ginza district, with its wood-paneled walls and worn-in leather reading chairs. It's an escape from Singapore's ultra-modernity that tends to inform other local establishments."

—Russel Wong, photographer

WHEN IN PORTO...

Nestled along the rocky edge of Matosinhos, just north of Porto, is the Michelin-starred **Casa de Chá da Boa Nova** (Avenida da Liberdade 1681), helmed by the chef Rui Paula and without question a most-perfect setting for a seafood lunch. Designed by the Pritzker Prize–winning architect Álvaro Siza, the historic 1956 structure was originally conceived as a teahouse. Pack your swimsuit, and after dining, stroll 15 minutes south to the **Leça Swimming Pool** complex, also designed by Siza, and bask in the serene scene. To round out your day of Siza, make a visit to the ethereal Siza-designed **Museu de Arte Contemporânea de Serralves** (Rua Dom João de Castro 210).

—The Editors

WHEN IN SINGAPORE...

Commanding a prime corner along Orchard Road, Singapore's toniest retail district, **Design Orchard** (250 Orchard Road) is an incubator and retail emporium designed by the firm WOHA that fosters nascent local designers and sells some 60-plus native brands including Silvia Teh's precision-cut separates and the Animal Project, a smile-inducing collection of tote bags, tees, and homewares illustrated by special-needs artists.

—The Editors

South Africa

The Manor House at Fancourt
Montagu Street, George, South Africa

Saxon Hotel, Villas & Spa
36 Saxon Road Sandhurst, Johannesburg, South Africa ↓

Shambala Private Game Reserve
Off R517, Vaalwater, South Africa

Thanda Safari Private Game Reserve
D242, Off the N2, Hluhluwe, KwaZulu Natal, South Africa

PRO TIP: MADRID

"Located just a few blocks from the Gran Hotel Inglés, Justicia has emerged as my favorite neighborhood in Madrid—and it's in the midst of a full boom. I love that it's just bursting with energy and projects. In Justicia, there is everything I like: food, clothes, a green market, and most importantly, galleries with international contemporary art programs. My favorite is **Travesia Cuatro** (Calle San Mateo 16), which has a roster of emerging and established artists like Donna Huanca and Álvarez Urbano."

—Rodman Primack, art adviser, co-owner of AGO Projects, and principal of the of the design firm RP Miller

Hotel Fenix, a Gran Meliá Hotel
Hermosilla, 2, Madrid, Spain

Hotel Las Arenas
Calle Eugenia Vines, 22–24, Valencia, Spain

Hotel Puente Romano Beach Resort
Bulevar Principe Alfonso von Hohenlohe, s/n, Marbella, Spain

La Bobadilla, A Royal Hideaway Hotel
Finca La Bobadilla, Carretera Salinas, Villanueva de Tapia, Km. 65.5, Loja, Granada, Spain

Majestic Hotel & Spa Barcelona
Passeig de Gràcia, 68, Barcelona, Spain

Marbella Club Hotel
Bulevar Principe Alfonso von Hohenlohe, s/n, Marbella, Spain ↓

ME Ibiza
Avenida de s'Argamassa, 153, Santa Eulalia del Rio, Ibiza, Spain

Palacio Arriluce Hotel (page 226)
C/Atxekolandeta 15, Getxo, Bilbao, Spain ↓

Palacio de los Duques, a Gran Meliá Hotel
Cuesta de Santo Domingo 5 y 7, Madrid, Spain

Seaside Grand Hotel Residencia
Avenida del Oasis, 32 Maspalomas, Gran Canaria, Spain

Villa Le Blanc, a Gran Meliá Hotel
Playa de Santo Tomás s/n, Menorca, Spain

(page 226)

PRO TIP: ST. MORITZ

"There may be chicer après-ski spots in the picturesque town, but **Hanselmann** (Via Maistra 8), the bakery and chocolate shop founded in 1894, is the most famous. The café, whose historic façade was restored in the 1980s, is a de facto meeting spot for residents and tourists alike, partially due to its central location on the main street next to the St. Mauritius Fountain. Come for a hot chocolate and *berliner*, and then shop for chocolate versions of snowballs and skis for loved ones back home.

"Since it was founded in 1974 by the famed playboy Gunter Sachs, **Dracula's Ghost Riders Club** (Via Maistra 54) has long been the see-and-be-seen nightclub in the Engadin. In recent years, the members-only spot has been known not just for its late-night antics, but also as a place where titans of industry hang with other like-minded moguls."

—Whitney Robinson, entrepreneur and editor

PRO TIP: MARBELLA

"Not far from the hotel is Marbella's historic old town, with its narrow streets, white-washed buildings, and delightful shops. I love getting lost in its charm and wrapping up the day at local tapas spots like **Taberna La Niña del Pisto** (C. San Lázaro, 1) or **Taberna Casa Curro** (C. Pantaleón, 7). Also stop by **Heladería La Valenciana** (Av. de Nabeul, 3) for ice cream or **Churrería Ramón** (Plaza de los Naranjos, 8). You also can't miss the nearby city of Málaga, where the **Museo Picasso Málaga** (Palacio de Buenavista, C. San Agustín, 8) and **Centre Pompidou Málaga** (Pje. del Dr. Carrillo Casaux, s/n) are treats for art lovers. As are the stunning cathedral **Alcazaba** (C/ Alcazabilla, 2) and the **Teatro Romano de Málaga** (C/ Alcazabilla, s/n).

"I enjoy reconnecting with nature by exploring the **Juanar Forest** or hiking up to the majestic **La Concha** peak, which shelters Marbella and provides its characteristic microclimate. Marbella's location is perfect for day trips to the laid-back, paradisiacal beaches of **Tarifa** or to Ronda's wineries for a wine-tasting adventure. My favorites are **Cortijo Los Aguilares** (Ctra. Campillos, Km. 35), **Bodega Doña Felisa** (Cordel del Puerto al Quejigal, s/n), and **F. Schatz** (Finca Sanguijuela, s/n)."

—Julián Cabanillas, general manager, Marbella Club Hotel

Sweden

Grand Hôtel Stockholm
Sodra Blasieholmshamnen 8, Stockholm, Sweden

Switzerland

Badrutt's Palace Hotel
Via Serlas 27, St. Moritz, Switzerland

Baur au Lac
Talstrasse 1, Zurich, Switzerland

Beau-Rivage Genève
13, Quai du Mont-Blanc, Geneva, Switzerland

Beau-Rivage Palace
Pace du Port 17–19, Lausanne, Switzerland

Bellevue Palace Bern
Kochergrasse 3–5, Bern, Switzerland

PRO TIP: LAUSANNE

"Nearby the Beau-Rivage Palace, you can find the **Aquatis Aquarium Vivarium** (Route de Berne 144). Occasionally, I enjoy escaping the manicured city to be among this collection of rare sea creatures. One of the highlights is the fully immersive tunnel pathway that cuts through the largest tank. Sharks and various fish swim overhead and up front. Sometimes you can forget that you're not actually a part of their world."

—Ini Archibong, designer

Bürgenstock Hotel & Alpine Spa
Bürgenstock Resort, Obbürgen, Switzerland ↓

Carlton Hotel St. Moritz
Via Johannes Badrutt 11, St. Moritz, Switzerland

Chalet RoyAlp Hotel & Spa
Domaine de Rochegrise, Villars-sur-Ollon, Switzerland

The Chedi Andermatt (page 157)
Gotthardstrasse 4, Andermatt, Switzerland ↓

PRO TIP: ST. MORITZ

"The shop **Ebneter & Biel** (Plazza dal Mulin 6) has been selling handmade linens since 1911. I love their hand-embroidered men's handkerchiefs and guest towels with winter motifs like skiers and mountain scenes that wouldn't be out of place under a mug of hot cocoa in Montana or a cut-crystal champagne flute after a day at the Cresta Run."

—Whitney Robinson, entrepreneur and editor

PRO TIP: BASEL

"I often stay at the Grand Hotel Trois Rois Basel with my daughter, and when we do, we love to venture out to see the latest exhibition at the **Fondation Beyeler** (Baselstrasse 101, Riehen). The Renzo Piano–designed museum is a place of tranquil exploration and houses an impressive collection featuring some of my favorite artists, like Ellsworth Kelly, Roni Horn, Wassily Kandinsky, and Picasso. Visiting is truly an escape. It's a wonderful place to introduce children to the greats. They also host a sunset rave every summer, which is not to be missed."

—Ini Archibong, designer

The Dolder Grand (page 158)
Kurhausstrasse 65, Zurich, Switzerland

Grand Hotel Les Trois Rois Basel
Blumenrain 8, Basel, Switzerland

Grand Resort Bad Ragaz
Bernard Simon-Strasse, Bad Ragaz, Switzerland

PRO TIP: ZURICH

"Inside the **University of Zurich's Law Faculty building** (Rämistrasse 74), originally designed by Hermann Fietz in 1909, lies an oval wonder designed by Santiago Calatrava. Previously an empty courtyard of the original chemistry building, the atrium now boasts a seven-story library of bright timber galleries that feature 16,400 feet (5,000 meters) of the school's rare books, as well as five hundred working spaces. This architectural masterpiece from 2004 is a stunning example of fusing historic, untouched exteriors with functional interiors for students, faculty, and visitors alike."

—Marguita Kracht, hotelier, Baur au Lac

PRO TIP: GSTAAD

"The **Grand Chalet of Rossinière** (Le Borjoz 12, Rossinière) is one of the largest and oldest chalets in Switzerland, dating to the eighteenth century and classed as a historic monument. In 1852, it was turned into a hotel, patronized by Europeans including Victor Hugo, as well as by Americans, Russians, and Australians. The painter Balthus bought it in 1977, welcoming his artist friends there until his death in 2001. These days, anyone can visit the nearby **Balthus Chapel** (1658 Rossinière), with its film installation by the director Wim Wenders."

—Andrea Scherz, general manager, Gstaad Palace

Gstaad Palace
Palacestrasse 28, Gstaad, Switzerland

Guarda Golf Hotel & Residences
Route des Zirès 14, Crans Montana, Switzerland

Hôtel des Trois Couronnes & Destination Spa
49 Rue d'Italie, Vevey, Switzerland

Hotel Eden Roc, Ascona
Via Albarelle, Ascona, Switzerland

Hotel Schweizerhof Bern & Spa
Bahnhofplatz 11, Bern, Switzerland

Hotel Splendide Royal
7 Riva A. Caccia, Lugano, Switzerland

Kulm Hotel St. Moritz (page 191)
Via Veglia 18, St. Moritz, Switzerland

La Réserve Eden au Lac Zurich
Utoquai 45, Zurich, Switzerland

La Réserve Genève Hotel, Spa & Villa
301 Route de Lausanne Bellevue, Geneva, Switzerland

Lausanne Palace
7-9, Rue du Grand-Chêne, Lausanne, Switzerland

LeCrans (page 208)
Chemin du Mont-Blanc 1, Plan Mayens, CP - 179, Crans-Montana, Switzerland ↓

Le Mirador Resort and Spa
Chemin de l'Hotel Mirador, 5, Le Mont-Pelerin, Switzerland

Mont Cervin Palace
Bahnhofstrasse 31, Zermatt, Switzerland

Park Gstaad
Wispilentrasse 29, Gstaad, Switzerland

Park Hotel Vitznau
Seestrasse 18, Vitznau, Switzerland

Riffelalp Resort 2222m
3920 Zermatt, Zermatt, Switzerland

Royal Savoy Hotel & Spa Lausanne
Avenue d'Ouchy, 40, Lausanne, Switzerland

"Along the iconic promenade of Gstaad lies the historic **Pernet Comestibles** (Promenade 75), dating from its original inception in 1904. The specialty market has continuously improved throughout the decades and now provides deliveries to nearly one third of Switzerland. Inside the picturesque market, you'll find delicately packaged teas and chocolates, caviar, and spectacular regional specialties like herbs, confits, truffles, wine, and spirits. Also worth stepping in for a visit while shopping along the Gstaad promenade is the beautiful **St. Nikolaus Kapelle** (Promenade 59), built in 1402 with its modern (fifteenth-century) stained glass and minimal religious adornments. Notable pieces to mention include the recently renovated organ, which is put to use on the second Sunday of every month, and the impeccable oak benches."

—Beverly Nguyen, boutique owner and fashion stylist

PRO TIP: ST. MORITZ

"There is no better place to buy sumptuous cashmere in vibrant hues and subtle shades of greige than at **Extreme Cashmere** (Via Somplaz 7). The Amsterdam-based brand known for its minimalist aesthetic linked up with the German design firm Apropos The Concept Store to create this serene space where sleek wooden shelves and sliding doors display everything from the label's cult-favorite sweaters to washing machines with instructions on proper textile care."

—Christina Ohly Evans, U.S. correspondent, *HTSI*

Suvretta House
Via Chasellas 1, St. Moritz, Switzerland

Tschuggen Grand Hotel, Arosa (page 246)
Sonnenbergstrasse, Arosa, Switzerland ↓

Victoria-Jungfrau Grand Hotel & Spa
Hoheweg 41, Interlaken, Switzerland

Widder Hotel (page 256)
Rennweg 7, Zurich, Switzerland

Tanzania

Thanda Island
Shungimbili Island, District of Mafia Island, Tanzania

Thailand

Aleenta Phuket – Phang Nga Resort & Spa
33, Khok Kloi, Takua Thung District, Phang-nga, Thailand

Aleenta Retreat Chiang Mai
189,189/1–6 Moo 14, Tambon Suthep, Chiang Mai, Thailand ↓

WHEN IN BANGKOK...

Look for the wing-tipped, mirror-clad roof of **Thai Home Industries** (35 Charoenkrung Soi 40), a cavernous space filled with the kingdom's rich craft and design heritage, and operated by the son and daughter of the late Jaivid Rangthong, who left the handles of his handmade stainless-steel utensils unpolished, inspired by upcountry Thai farm tools used to slash through verdant rice paddies.

—The Editors

PRO TIP: ZURICH

"Delve into the comprehensive **Museum of Design Zurich** (Pfingstweidstrasse 96), which holds 500,000-plus historical objects and ephemera—everything from the classic Swiss Army knife by Victorinox and vintage posters to the original Helvetica typeface. Set in two locations, the primary collection is housed in a listed 1930s building that's a must-see example of modernist Swiss architecture."

—Christina Ohly Evans, U.S. correspondent, *HTSI*

Capella Bangkok
300/2 Charoenkrung Road,
Yannawa, Sathorn, Bangkok, Thailand

The Nai Harn (page 101)
23/3 Moo 1 Vises Road, Rawai,
Muang District, Phuket, Thailand ↓

The Okura Prestige Bangkok
57 Wireless Road, Bangkok,
Thailand

Raya Heritage
157 Moo 6, Tambol Donkaew
Amphur, Mae Rim, Chiang Mai,
Thailand

Rayavadee
214 Moo 2, Tambon, Ao-Nang,
Amphur Muang, Krabi, Thailand

PRO TIP: BANGKOK

"**Charmgang** (14, 35
Charoenkrung Road) in the old
Chinatown district of Bangkok
offers contemporary Thai cuisine. The menu changes monthly,
but always focuses on the chefs'
specialties—grilled dishes,
yummy salads, and exceptional
curries. The curated selection of
cocktails and natural wines and
the bold, graphic interior lend a
movie-scene vibe."

—Kulapat Yantrasast, architect

Tunisia

La Badira
BP N°437 Route Touristique
Hammamet Nord, Hammamet,
Tunisia

Turkey

Bodrum Loft
Golkoy Region 78, Main Road 325,
Street No. 7, Bodrum, Turkey ↓

**Çırağan Palace Kempinski
Istanbul**
Çırağan Caddesi, No. 32, Besiktas,
Istanbul, Turkey

D Maris Bay
Datca Road, 35 Km., Hisaronu
Village, Marmaris, Mugla, Turkey

Maxx Royal Bodrum Resort
Golkoy Mah. 312 Sk., No. 3, Bodrum,
Turkey

Maxx Royal Kemer Resort
Kiris Mh., Kiris Cad. No. 88, Kemer,
Antalya, Turkey

**The Montgomerie Golf Club by
Maxx Royal Resorts**
Belek Mah. Günübirlik Caddesi
Maxx Royal Otel, No, 2/A, Serik,
Belek, Turkey

WHEN IN ISTANBUL...

In their high-ceilinged, herringbone-
floored 19th-century atelier just off
Taksim Square, twin sisters Ayca
and Zeynep Sadikoglu make **OYE
Swimwear** (Inönü Caddesi 27/2
Gumussuyu), highly structured
bikinis and one-piece bathing suits
that elevate the category far beyond
basic triangles. The pieces are named
for the sisters' quirky interests in
classic films, cartoon superheroes,
and science fiction.

—The Editors

Turks and Caicos Islands

Grace Bay Club
Grace Bay Circle Road,
Providenciales, Turks and Caicos
Islands

Rock House (page 77)
1 Blue Mountain Road,
Providenciales,
Turks and Caicos Islands ↓

Wymara Resort and Villas
Lower Bight Road, Providenciales,
Turks and Caicos Islands

Ukraine

Opera Hotel
53, B. Khmelnitskogo Street, Kyiv,
Ukraine

PRO TIP: LONDON

"A fresh, welcoming perspective to the experimental omakase contributions within London's Westminster radius, **Taku Mayfair** (36 Albemarle Street) holds a Michelin star for good reason. Interiors within the sixteen-seat omakase are formed from skillfully treated lacquered and waxed woods, while internal slate façades offset warm, supple lighting. The experience is both intimate and open, due to the proximity to the counter. Fundamentally, this creates a rhythmic dining experience centered around chef Takuya Watanabe's literacy relating to the physical formation and actions relevant to each dish. Ushering in joy and anticipation, each masterful serving awaits the fortunate guests."

—Samuel Ross, artist and fashion designer

WHEN IN LONDON...

Around the corner from L'oscar London is one of the most majestic spaces in the world: the **Sir John Soane's Museum** (13 Lincoln's Inn Fields). This meticulously kept house and museum of the British architect Sir John Soane (1753–1837), who was well known for his Neoclassical structures and inventive use of light, bestows a quiet power upon those who enter. Inside the crowded but gracefully and purposefully curated galleries across three conjoined buildings are thousands of objects— paintings, antiquities, furniture, sculptures, and architectural models and drawings—still organized just as Soane intended.

—The Editors

United States

PRO TIP: MALIBU

"A National Historic Site just a few minutes' walk from Malibu Beach Inn, **Adamson House** (23200 Pacific Coast Highway) was constructed in 1928. Thanks to its acquisition first by Franciscan monks and then the state of California, its hand-carved teakwood doors, hand-painted murals, molded ceilings, hand-wrought ironwork, and lead-framed bottle glass windows remain perfectly preserved, as if a hundred years have not passed."

—Gregory Day, president, Mani Brothers Real Estate Group

PRO TIP: LOS ANGELES

"Just up the hill from the Pacific Coast Highway sits the **Eames House** (203 Chautauqua Boulevard), also known as Case Study House No. 8. Designed and built by Ray and Charles Eames in 1949, it's a Midcentury Modern landmark. They were commissioned to build it as a case study, but ended up moving in and living there for the rest of their lives. Have a picnic under the eucalyptus trees overlooking the Pacific Ocean or tour the interiors, filled with their collections of Isamu Noguchi Akari lamps, Native American baskets, and art from around the world."

—Kate Berry, chief creative officer, *Domino* magazine

PRO TIP: BOSTON

"A hidden treasure, the **Boston Athenaeum** ($10\frac{1}{2}$ Beacon Street) is a library and museum like no other. Built in 1807 and spread across five light-filled floors, the collection comprises half a million volumes, including George Washington's library, as well as rare maps and manuscripts. Attend an author talk or go on an art and architecture tour—you won't be disappointed."

—Christina Ohly Evans, U.S. correspondent, *HTSI*

The Setai, Miami Beach (page 78)
2001 Collins Avenue, Miami Beach, Florida, United States ↓

Sonnenalp Hotel
20 Vail Road, Vail, Colorado, United States

Villa Mara Carmel
2408 Bay View Avenue, Carmel-by-the-Sea, California, United States

Washington School House Hotel
543 Park Avenue, Park City, Utah, United States

The Whitfield Las Olas Hotel & Spa
1007 East Las Olas Boulevard, Fort Lauderdale, Florida, United States

Uruguay

Hotel Montevideo
José Benito Lamas 2901, Montevideo, Uruguay

Venezuela

Cayena-Caracas
Av. Don Eugenio Mendoza Entre Calles Jose Angel Lamas y El Bosque, La Castellana, Caracas, Venezuela

Zimbabwe

The Victoria Falls Hotel
1 Mallet Drive, Victoria Falls, Zimbabwe

Contributors

Jolanta Alberty is this book's photo editor. Previously, she was the senior visuals editor at *GQ* and *GQ Style* magazines, where she collaborated with various photographers and artists, creating award-winning images recognized by the American Society of Magazine Editors, the Society of Publication Designers, and *American Illustration–American Photography*. Alberty joined the curator and critic Hilton Als as a photo editor on several exhibitions, including "Toni Morrison's Black Book" at David Zwirner. She is based in Rhode Island.

Spencer Bailey is the editor-in-chief of The Leading Hotels of the World book series. A writer, editor, and journalist, he is the co-founder of the New York–based media company The Slowdown and the host of the Time Sensitive podcast. Bailey has contributed to publications such as *Bloomberg Businessweek*, *Fortune*, *The New York Times Magazine*, and *Town & Country*, and from 2013 to 2018, he was the editor-in-chief of *Surface* magazine. He is the author of several books, including *In Memory Of: Designing Contemporary Memorials* (Phaidon), and co-chair of the board of trustees of the Noguchi Museum in Long Island City, New York. In 2023, he was named to the *Wallpaper* USA 300 list of "talents that are forging new paths through America's design landscape."

Ramon Broza is the head of production and operations at The Slowdown, and oversees production of The Leading Hotels of the World book series. As a producer, he has worked on projects spanning the globe, including production for CNN and MTV, production management for Live Nation, and content creation for clients such as Nike and Cardi B.

Elizabeth Daniels is a Los Angeles–based architectural and editorial photographer. Her 2021 solo exhibition "For Edith" was shown at the Edith Farnsworth House, designed by Mies van der Rohe. Her photos of John Lautner's Hope House were featured in a 2023 exhibition at the Art, Design & Architecture Museum in California. Daniels's photos have appeared in publications including *Architectural Digest*, *The New York Times*, *The Wall Street Journal*, *Condé Nast Traveler*, and *Wallpaper*. She has been the recipient of three American Institute of Architects Architectural Photography Awards.

Maria Cristina Didero is a Milan-based independent design curator, consultant, and author. The curatorial director of the Design Miami fair, she has also curated numerous exhibitions for institutions around the world, including "Nendo: The Space in Between at Design" at Israel's Design Museum Holon and "Fun House" by Snarkitecture at National Building Museum in Washington, D.C. Her writing has appeared in magazines such as *Apartamento*, *Domus*, *L'Officiel*, and *Vogue Italia*. She was editor-at-large of *Icon Design* from 2018 to 2020, and now serves as the Milan editor of *Wallpaper*.

Mark Ellwood is a British-born, New York–based travel journalist. A contributing editor to *Condé Nast Traveler* and an editor-at-large for *Robb Report*, he is also a columnist for Bloomberg Luxury, and the creator and co-host of Bloomberg's Travel Genius podcast. Ellwood also contributes to *The Wall Street Journal* and *The New York Times*, and is a regular guest on NBC's *Today* show.

Paul Goldberger is an architecture critic, educator, and writer. A contributing editor for *Vanity Fair*, he was awarded the Pulitzer Prize for distinguished criticism at *The New York Times* and was previously the architecture critic for *The New Yorker*.

Brooke Hodge is a curator and writer based in Palm Springs, California, whose practice focuses on the intersections between architecture, art, and other forms of design, including fashion, product, and graphics. With more than thirty-five years of museum experience, she has held senior curatorial and administrative positions at institutions including the Palm Springs Art Museum; the Cooper Hewitt, Smithsonian Design Museum in New York; the Hammer Museum in Los Angeles; and Harvard University's Graduate School of Design.

Emily Jiang is the senior editor at The Slowdown. Prior to working at The Slowdown, she was the founder and editor-in-chief of the philosophy journal *Tabula Rasa* at Pomona College. She is a graduate of the Columbia Publishing Course.

Gaelle Le Boulicaut is a Brittany- and Paris-based photographer with an extensive background in portraiture and interiors. Her work has appeared in magazines including *Architectural Digest*, *Condé Nast Traveler*, *Elle Décor*, and *Le Figaro*. She studied photography at Université Laval in Canada and at the Australian Centre for Photography in Sydney.

Hazen Mayo is a former editorial assistant at The Slowdown, and has worked in communications roles at Roman and Williams Buildings and Interiors, the Brooklyn Museum, and Sutton. A graduate of Yale University, she is currently a postbaccalaureate psychology student at Columbia University.

Ogata is a Tokyo-born, New York–based photographer. He has taken portraits of cultural luminaries such as Tadao Ando, Thom Browne, Larry Gagosian, Selena Gomez, Yayoi Kusama, Bill Nighy, Joseph Stiglitz, and Yohji Yamamoto, among others, and his work has appeared in publications including *GQ*, *Vanity Fair*, and *Vogue*.

Christina Ohly Evans is the U.S. correspondent for the *Financial Times*'s *HTSI*. She previously served as an editor for Daily Candy in both New York and London, and also as a vice president of creative content for iVillage and Oxygen Media.

Cynthia Rosenfeld is the executive editor of the LHW book series. The editor-at-large of The Slowdown, she began her international writing career as the Asia editor for *Condé Nast Traveler*, where she continues to contribute to this day. Her work has also appeared in the *Financial Times*'s *HTSI*, *The New York Times*, *Robb Report*, *Travel+Leisure*, and *Wallpaper*, among other publications.

Warren Singh-Bartlett has worked as a journalist and television writer in Lebanon, Dubai, Seville, and the United Kingdom. Before moving to Beijing in 2020, where he now works as a features editor at *China Daily*, he was *Wallpaper*'s Middle East editor for 20 years. He is the author of two books about Lebanon and four guides in the *Wallpaper City Guides* series from Phaidon.

Frederik Vercruysse is an Antwerp-based photographer known for his minimalist, ethereal style. His work has been shown at exhibitions in Antwerp and Brussels, and he has worked with clients including Diptyque, Hermès, Molteni&C, Muller Van Severen, Raf Simons, Vincent Van Duysen, and Zara Home. Vercruysse's photographs have been published in magazines such as *Architectural Digest*, *Le Monde D'Hermès*, *T: The New York Times Style Magazine*, *Wallpaper*, and *WSJ Magazine*.

Russel Wong is a Singapore-based photographer who began his career in Los Angeles, shooting for fashion magazines such as *Vogue* and *Elle*. His photographs have appeared on the cover of *Time* magazine 17 times to date, and he has taken portraits of celebrities such as Richard Gere, Jackie Chan, Michelle Yeoh, and Barack Obama. He has also worked with Oscar-winning directors including Ang Lee and Zhang Yimou, and has created images for the movie posters for films such as *Crouching Tiger, Hidden Dragon* (2000); *House of Flying Daggers* (2004); and *Lust Caution* (2007).

Janelle Zara is a Los Angeles–based freelance journalist whose work can be found in several publications beginning with "art" (*Artnet*, *Artforum*, *ARTnews*, and the *Art Newspaper*), as well as in the *Guardian*, *T: The New York Times Style Magazine*, and others. She is the author of the book *Becoming an Architect*.

Acknowledgments

The Leading Hotels of the World would like to thank Andrea Scherz, the chairman of LHW's Executive Committee, and the other Executive Committee board members—Lynne Biggar, Guido Fiorentino, Ruth Jones, Richard Leuenberger, Peter Shaindlin, Matthias Winkler, and Deborah Yager-Fleming—for believing in and supporting this book series. LHW would also like to thank all our member hotels for their collaboration, and for making this book a complete joy to put together. Extra thanks to the hotels that welcomed our team for the book's feature stories and interviews: Ambiente, A Landscape Hotel; Botanic Sanctuary Antwerp; Casa Polanco; The Greenwich Hotel; La Réserve Paris – Hotel and Spa; The Okura Tokyo; and Portrait Milano.

The Slowdown would like to thank The Leading Hotels of the World team, in particular Shannon Knapp, Phil Koserowski, Lauren Alba, Susan Ziluca, Gina Anderson, Michael Fragoso, and Lauren Ingram. Thanks, too, to Keith Fox, Philip Ruppel, Michael Vagnetti, Sean Newcott, and Holly La Due at Phaidon and Monacelli, and to Michael Bierut and Laitsz Ho at Pentagram. We would also like to give special acknowledgement to Jolanta Alberty, this book's photo editor, who worked tirelessly to gather and track down the beautiful imagery in these pages. Thanks also go to Mimi Hannon, who tightened up the texts with her ace copy edits. Finally, a huge thank you to the project's many writers and photographers: Elizabeth Daniels, Maria Cristina Didero, Mark Ellwood, Gaelle Le Boulicaut, Paul Goldberger, Hazen Mayo, Ogata, Christina Ohly Evans, Warren Singh-Bartlett, Frederik Vercruysse, Russel Wong, and Janelle Zara. This is a dream project, with a dream team to boot.

Spencer Bailey would like to thank Sam Bhadha, a hotelier who in my late adolescent years opened me up to the wonders of the hospitality trade and showed me the inner workings of what makes a great hotel tick. Sam lit a hospitality fire in me that's still burning to this day. I would also like to thank Shinji Umehara, Kenji Takayanagi, Satomi Sakaguchi, Kaori Wakui, Yuzo Uchiyama, and Takashi Usuba for the incredibly generous hospitality during my stay at The Okura Tokyo. I will never forget it. And special thanks to Michael Bierut and Laitsz Ho at Pentagram—following *In Memory Of*, it's an absolute pleasure to be working together on another book project. Thanks also to Carla Fernández, Gabriela Hearst, Daniel Humm, and Michel Rojkind for being a part of this adventure, and to Paul Goldberger for writing this book's beautiful foreword. Lastly, I would like to thank Jolanta, Ramon, Adriana, Mimi, Emily, and Cynthia for being the absolute best colleagues and collaborators I could ever ask for.

Cynthia Rosenfeld would like to thank Sandrine Versavel, Sven Klockaerts, Xavier Le Clef, Kristl Bakermans Le Bon, Rebecca Verstraete, and Tanguy Ottomer for sharing the delights of Botanic Sanctuary Antwerp and its surrounding enchantments. *Merci mille fois* to Aurore Cornic and Marie-France Grégoire for revealing what makes La Réserve Paris a veritable fairy tale, and to Edouard Delavaux for *le chocolat chaud*. Throughout my travels across Asia, Europe, North Africa, and the Americas, legendary hoteliers have granted me unparalleled access to their magnificent properties, along with lessons in luxury hospitality priceless to any pursuit, personal or professional. I am grateful to each and every one of them. Finally, my deepest gratitude to Spencer for inviting me on this excellent adventure and for the opportunity to work with such a talented team.

Credits

Image & Art Credits

T—top, B—bottom, C—center, L—left, and R—right

2, 140, 143–44, 146–47, 149, 260: Frederik Vercruysse; Quadriga Management Artists & Production; **10–13:** Courtesy Christos Drazos; **20–21, 22:** Courtesy Yellow Box Drone; **23:** Courtesy Troy Campbell; **24, 27–28, 30–33:** Elizabeth Daniels; **34, 37–38, 41–42, 44, 47–48, 51, 52:** Ogata; **34:** (sculpture, L) Juan Pablo Vidal, *Lost letter to Santa Claus*, Courtesy Juan Pablo Vidal; **41 L:** (painting) Jordi Boldo, *Evoked Landscape*, from the series *The imperative of the gaze*; Courtesy Jordi Boldo; **41 R:** (photographs, L to R) Graciela Iturbide, *Saguaro, Sonoran Desert*, 1979, silver gelatin print, 14 × 11 in. (35.6 × 27.9 cm); *El baño de Frida [Frida´s Bathroom], Coyoacán, Mexico City*, 2005, silver gelatin print, 20 × 16 in. (50.8 × 40.6 cm); Courtesy Graciela Iturbide; **54–55:** Courtesy Brandan Barré; **55:** (collage) Stefan Gunnesch, collage on paper and acrylic digital print, 90 × 68 in. (228.6 × 172.7 cm), Courtesy Stefan Gunnesch/BILDSCHRIFTLICH; (sculpture, foreground) Will Robinson, *Sistine Bench*, basalt, 48 × 19 × 31 in. (121.9 × 48.3 × 78.7 cm), 2006, Courtesy Will Robinson and Bau-Xi Gallery; **59:** Courtesy JP Piter; **66–67:** Courtesy Brice Ferre; **68:** Courtesy Douglas Friedman and The Newbury Boston; **69 T:** Courtesy The Newbury Boston; **69 B:** Courtesy Nikolas Koenig and The Newbury Boston; **70–71:** Courtesy The Newbury Boston; **72–73:** Courtesy Stephen Kent Johnson; **78–79:** Courtesy The Setai, Miami Beach; **90 T:** (sculpture) Bernar Venet, *219.5° Arc x 22*, 2006, Cor-ten steel, site-specific installation footprint, height: 141.7 in. (360 cm), diameter: 14 ft. 1 19/64 in. (430 cm) © 2024 Bernar Venet, Artists Rights Society (ARS), New York / ADAGP, Paris; **95 B:** Frank Lloyd Wright(R) Suite, © 2024 Frank Lloyd Wright Foundation. All Rights Reserved. Licensed by Artists Rights Society (ARS), New York; **96–99:** Courtesy Lohkah Hotel & Spa and Jonathan Leijonhufvud; **102, 105–06, 108–11:** Russel Wong; **106 T:** (chandelier) © Lina Ghotmeh – Architecture; **112:** Li Jingbin, *Black and White Beauties*, Courtesy of Li Jingbin; **122–23:** Courtesy Jerome Galland; **132–35:** Courtesy Benjamin Antony Monn; **144 TL:** Nick Ervinck, *NARTUAT*, 2020, iron, polyester and polyurethane, 92.9 × 59 × 41.3 in. (236 × 150 × 105 cm), Courtesy Studio Nick Ervinck and NQ Gallery, Copyright: Studio Nick Ervinck; **152–53:** Courtesy Umberto D'Aniello and Gianni De Gennaro; **160–61:** (sculpture, BR) Duane Hanson, *Traveller*, 1985-87, bronze polychromed in oil, found clothing, hair, duffel bag and sleeping bag, wooden sticks and paper tickets, figure: 32 × 47 × 27 in. (81.3 × 119.4 × 68.8 cm), installation dimensions variable © 2024 Estate of Duane Hanson / Licensed by VAGA at Artists Rights Society (ARS), NY; (painting, TR) Andy Warhol, *Big Retrospective Painting*, © 2024 The Andy Warhol Foundation for the Visual Arts, Inc. / Licensed by Artists Rights Society (ARS), New York. Marilyn Monroe™; Rights of Publicity and Persona Rights are used with permission of The Estate of Marilyn Monroe LLC.; (painting, R) Bob and Roberta Smith, *Envy*, 2009, Courtesy Bob and Roberta Smith; (painting, CTR) Urs Fischer, *Bromine*, 2015, aluminum panel, aramid honeycomb, two-component polyurethane adhesive, two-component epoxy primer, galvanized steel rivet nuts, acrylic primer, gesso, acrylic ink, acrylic silkscreen medium, acrylic paint, 80 × 60 × ⅞ in. (203.2 × 152.4 × 2.2 cm) © Urs Fischer; (B, far R) Igor Baskakov, *Triumph* © Igor Baskakov; **182, 183 T:** Courtesy Will Pryce; **183 B:** Courtesy Studio Phenix Monaco; **184:** Courtesy Sara Magni; **185:** Courtesy JP Piter; **190–93:** Courtesy Kulm Hotel St. Moritz; **196, 199–200, 203–05:** Courtesy Gaelle Le Boulicaut; **212:** Courtesy Yann Allegre; **213 T:** Courtesy Marc Berenguer; (framed photograph, CL) © Yann Allegre; **213 B:** (paintings) © Philippe Icher; **214–15:** Courtesy Lido Palace; **218–19:** © Eames Office, LLC. All rights reserved; **220–23:** Courtesy Pellicano Hotels; **226–29:** Courtesy Belén Martinez Imaz; **230, 234, 236–39:** Courtesy Portrait Milano; **233:** Courtesy Daria Klepikova; **242–43:** Courtesy Jerome Galland; **244, 245 B:** Courtesy Matthieu Salvaing; **245 T:** Danilo Scarpati; **252–53:** Courtesy Villa Nai 3.3; **256 B, 257, 258–59:** Courtesy Stefania Giorgi/The Living Circle; **264 L:** (Fauchon L'Hôtel Paris) Courtesy of Gilles TRILLARD; **265 T:** (Bayerischer Hof) Courtesy of Benjamin Monn; **273 C:** (Hotel Metropole Monte-Carlo) Courtesy of Will Pryce; **275 L:** (São Lourenço do Barrocal) Courtesy of Ash James; **275 R:** (Le Sereno Hotel, Villas & Spa) Courtesy of Emily Lab; **281:** (Acqualina Resort & Residences on the Beach) Courtesy of Troy Campbell; **282 R:** (Nine Orchard) Courtesy of Stephen Kent Johnson.

Library of Library of Congress Control Number: 2024933240
ISBN 978-1-58093-655-2
10 9 8 7 6 5 4 3 2 1

Printed in China

Design by Pentagram

Monacelli
A Phaidon Company
111 Broadway
New York, NY 10006
monacellipress.com

The Leading Hotels of the World
485 Lexington Ave
New York, NY 10017
lhw.com